A SELF-STUDY COURSE ON
POLITICAL ISLAM
LEVEL 3

A THREE LEVEL COURSE

BILL WARNER, EDITOR

A SELF-STUDY COURSE ON
POLITICAL ISLAM
LEVEL 3

A THREE LEVEL COURSE

BILL WARNER, EDITOR

ISBN13   978-1-936659-11-1

V 06.13.11

PUBLISHED BY CSPI, LLC
WWW.CSPIPUBLISHING.COM

PRINTED IN THE USA

TABLE OF CONTENTS

MEDITER-
RANEAN
SEA

SYRIA

MAP OF
ARABIA
600 A.D.

MESOPOTAMIA
(IRAQ)

•MUTA

•TABUK

•FADAK
•KHAYBAR

ARABIA

•MEDINA

•BADR

R E D   S E A

•MECCA
•HUDABIYA
•HUNAIN

EGYPT

YEMEN

N

ABYSSINIA
(ETHIOPIA)

INTRODUCTION
LESSON 1

THIS BOOK

This book is the third in a series of lessons devoted to the study of Political Islam. Each book has a discussion of the same lessons on different aspects of Islam, so you get to study the same subject at three different levels. However, you could pick up any of the three levels and understand it.

A full introduction is given in Level 1. However, since each of the three levels can stand on its own, the following is a brief summary of the introduction in Level 1.

The scientific method is a new approach to the study of Islam. Analysis shows that Islam is both a religion and a political system, and that the political system is the greatest part of Islamic doctrine.

THE TRILOGY

The Trilogy is made up of three books—

• The Koran is what Mohammed reported as the message from Allah. But the Koran does not contain enough guidance for one to be a Muslim. The Koran repeatedly says that all of the world should imitate Mohammed in every way. Mohammed's words and deeds are called the Sunna. The Sunna is found in two different texts—the Sira and Hadith.

• The first source of the Sunna is the Sira which is Mohammed's biography.

• The other source of the Sunna is the Hadith, the Traditions of Mohammed. There are several versions of Hadith, but the most commonly used is by Bukhari.

So the Trilogy is the Koran, Sira and Hadith. The Koran is the smallest part of Islam's "bible". It could be said that Islam is 16% Allah and 84% Mohammed.

1

All of the foundations of Islamic doctrine is found in the Trilogy. Once you know the Trilogy, you know all of the foundations of Islam.

KAFIR

The Koran says that the Kafir may be deceived, plotted against, hated, enslaved, mocked, tortured and worse. The word is usually translated as "unbeliever" but this translation is wrong. The word "unbeliever" is logically and emotionally neutral, whereas, Kafir is the most abusive, prejudiced and hateful word in any language.

There are many religious names for Kafirs: polytheists, idolaters, People of the Book (Christians and Jews), Buddhists, atheists, agnostics, and pagans. Kafir covers them all, because no matter what the religious name is, they can all be treated the same. What Mohammed said and did to polytheists can be done to any other category of Kafir.

Islam devotes a great amount of energy to the Kafir. The majority (64%) of the Koran is devoted to the Kafir, and nearly all of the Sira (81%) deals with Mohammed's struggle with them. The Hadith (Traditions) devotes 32% of the text to Kafirs[1]. Overall, the Trilogy devotes 60% of its content to the Kafir.

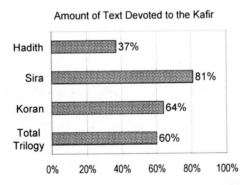

Amount of Text Devoted to the Kafir

POLITICAL ISLAM

What is the difference between religious Islam and Political Islam? Do you remember when some Danish artists drew some cartoons of Mohammed? There were weeks of rioting, threats, lawsuits, killings, assassinations and destruction by Muslims. If Muslims want to respect Mohammed by never criticizing, joking about him and taking every word he said as a

---

1   http://cspipublishing.com/statistical/TrilogyStats/AmtTxtDevoted-Kafir.html

sacred example—that is religious. But when they threaten, pressure and hurt Kafirs for not respecting Mohammed, that is political. When Muslims say that Mohammed is the prophet of the only god, that is religious, but when they insist that Kafirs never disrespect Mohammed, that is political. When the newspapers and TV agreed not to publish the cartoons, that was a political response, not a religious response.

THE THREE VIEWS OF ISLAM

There are three points of view relative to Islam. The point of view depends upon how you feel about Mohammed. If you believe Mohammed is the prophet of Allah, then you are a believer. If you don't, you are a Kafir. The third viewpoint is that of an apologist for Islam. Apologists do not believe that Mohammed was a prophet, but they are tolerant about Islam without any actual knowledge of Islam.

Here is an example of the three points of view.

In Medina, Mohammed sat all day long beside his 12-year-old wife while they watched as the heads of 800 Jews were removed by sword.[2] Their heads were cut off because they had said that Mohammed was not the prophet of Allah. Muslims view these deaths as necessary because denying Mohammed's prophet-hood was, and remains, an offense against Islam. They were beheaded because it is sanctioned by Allah.

Kafirs look at this event as proof of the jihadic violence of Islam and as an evil act.

Apologists say that this was an historic event; that all cultures have violence in their past, and no judgment should be passed. They have never actually read any of Islam's foundational texts, but speak authoritatively about Islam.

According to the different points of view, killing the 800 Jews was:

- A tragedy
- A perfect sacred act
- Another historical event. We have done worse.

There is no "right" view of Islam, since the views cannot be reconciled.

This book is written from the Kafir point of view. Everything in this book views Islam from the perspective of how Islam affects Kafirs. This also means that the religion is of little importance. A Muslim cares about the religion of Islam, but all Kafirs are affected by Islam's political views.

---

2   *The Life of Muhammad*, A. Guillaume, Oxford University Press, 1982, pg. 464.

We must talk about Islam in the political realm, because it is a powerful political system.

This is a fact-based study. You can read the actual doctrine for yourself and draw your own conclusions.

REFERENCE NUMBERS

The information in this book can be traced back to the source by use of the reference numbers:

Ishaq234 is a reference to Ibn Ishaq's *Sirat Rasul Allah*, translated by A. Guillaume as *The Life of Muhammad*. This is a reference to margin note 234. All of these references are condensed for ease of understanding.

Bukhari2,3,45 is a reference to *Sahih Bukhari*, Bukhari's Hadith. The three example numbers are volume 2, book 3, and number 45, a standard reference system.

Muslim2,345 is a reference to *Sahih Muslim*, Muslim's Hadith. The example would be book 2, number 345.

Koran12:45 is Koran chapter (sura) 12, verse 45.

GLOSSARY

There is a glossary of Islamic words in the very back.

THE SIRA—THE LIFE OF MOHAMMED

HIS FAMILY

Mohammed's father was called Abdullah, meaning slave of Allah. Allah was a high god of the many gods worshiped in the town of Mecca. Abdullah died while Mohammed's mother was pregnant. When he was five years old, his mother died and his grandfather took over his upbringing. Then Mohammed was orphaned for the third time when his grandfather died and his raising was assumed by his uncle, Abu Talib. All were of the Quraysh tribe. These brief facts are the only history known about his early childhood.

MARRIAGE

Ishaq120[1] Mohammed was grown when he was hired by the wealthy widow and a distant cousin, Khadija, to act as her agent in trading with Syria. Syria was a Christian nation with many Jews. Mohammed had a reputation of good character and good business sense. Trading from Mecca to Syria was risky business because it took skill to manage a caravan and then to make the best deal in Syria. He managed Khadija's affairs well, and she returned a good profit on the trading.

Ishaq120 Khadija was well known among the Quraysh tribe. Sometime after hiring Mohammed as her business agent, she proposed marriage to him. They married and had six children. Their two sons died in childhood, and the four daughters lived to adulthood.

Ishaq150 Mohammed would take month-long retreats to be alone and observe the Quraysh religious practices.

Ishaq152 At the age of forty, Mohammed began to have visions and hear voices. His visions were first shown to him as bright as daybreak during his sleep in the month of Ramadan. Mohammed said that the angel, Gabriel, came to him with a brocade with writing on it and commanded him to read. "What shall I read?" The angel pressed him and said, "Read."

---

1. Ishaq120 means that this comes from Ishaq, margin note 120.

5

Mohammed said again, "What shall I read?" The angel pressed him again tightly and again commanded, "Read!" Again the reply, "What shall I read?"

The angel said:

> Koran96:1 *Recite: In the name of your Lord, Who created man from clots of blood.*
>
> Koran96:3 *Recite: Your Lord is the most generous, Who taught the use of the pen and taught man what he did not know.*

T1150 Mohammed awoke from his sleep. Now Mohammed hated ecstatic poets and the insane. His thoughts were that he was now either a poet or insane, that which he hated. He thought to kill himself by jumping off a cliff. And off he went to do just that. Half way up the hill, he heard, "Mohammed, You are the apostle of Allah and I am Gabriel." He gazed at the angel and no matter which way he turned his head the vision followed his eyes. Mohammed stood there for a long time.

THE FIRST CONVERT

Ishaq156 Mohammed's wife, Khadija, was his first convert. From the first she had encouraged and believed him. She knew him to be of good character and did not think him to be deceived or crazy.

Soon he stopped hearing voices or seeing visions and became depressed and felt abandoned until his visions started again. Then Mohammed began to tell others who were close to him of the words in his visions.

THE FIRST MALES TO ACCEPT ISLAM

Ishaq160 Mohammed and Ali used to go to the edge of town to practice their new ritual prayers. One day Abu Talib came upon them and asked what they were doing. Mohammed replied, "Uncle, this is the religion of Allah, His angels, His prophets and the religion of Abraham. Allah has sent me as an apostle to all mankind. You, my uncle, deserve that I should teach you the truth and call you to Islam." His uncle said that he could not give up the religion of his ancestors, but that he would support Mohammed.

Ishaq161 A new element was added to the religion. Any person who rejected the revelations of Mohammed would be eternally punished. The culture of religious tolerance in Mecca now had a new religion which preached the end of tolerance. Only Islam was acceptable.

Mohammed preached a new doctrine in Mecca. After the Judgment Day would come Paradise and Hell.

Ishaq166 Since the word was out, Mohammed began to openly preach his new doctrine. He had been private for three years before he went public. While Mohammed was weak he preached tolerance:

> Koran73:10 *Listen to what they [Kafirs] say with patience, and leave them with dignity. Let me deal with the wealthy and those who deny the truth.*

Ishaq166 The Muslims went to the edge of Mecca to pray in order to be alone. One day a group of the Quraysh came upon them and began to mock them and a fight started. Saad, a Muslim, picked up the jaw bone of a camel and struck one of the Quraysh with it and bloodied him. This violence was the first blood to be shed in Islam.

Ishaq167 When Mohammed spoke about his new religion, it did not cause any problems among the Meccans. Then Mohammed began to condemn their religion and rituals and worship. This was a new phenomena. New religions could be added and had been, but not to the detriment of others. The Meccans took offense and resolved to treat him as an enemy. Luckily, he had the protection of his influential uncle, Abu Talib.

Ishaq168 Some of the Quraysh went to Abu Talib, Mohammed's tribal protector, and said to him, "Your nephew has cursed our gods, insulted our religion, mocked our way of life, criticized our civilization, attacked our virtues, and said that our forefathers were ignorant and in error. You must stop him, or you must let us stop him. We will rid you of him." Abu Talib gave them a soft reply and sent them away.

Ishaq169 The Quraysh saw that Abu Talib would not help. Mohammed continued to preach Islam and attack them and their lives. Mecca was a small town, everybody knew everybody. Islam had split the town of Mecca and divided the ruling and priestly tribe. The Quraysh were attacked at the very ground of their social being.

Ishaq170 Things got much worse. Now there was open hostility in the town. Quarrels increased, arguments got very heated. Complete disharmony dominated the town. The tribe started to abuse the recently converted Muslims. But Mohammed's uncle Abu Talib was a respected elder and was able to protect them from real harm.

PUBLIC TEACHING

At first Mohammed had only shared his message with close friends and relatives. Then he began to move more into the public. As Mohammed continued to preach Islam, more arguments occurred. More and more of the Koran began condemning those who disagreed with Mohammed's words. He preached that the only true religion was Islam and all of the Meccans were wrong and enemies of Allah. Mohammed's opponents were doomed to Hell. He cursed their gods, he denigrated their religion and divided the community, setting one tribesman against the others. The Quraysh felt that this was past all bearing. Tolerance had always been their way. Many clans, many gods, many religions. Another religion was acceptable, so why did Mohammed demean them?

MORE ARGUMENTS WITH THE MECCANS

Ishaq188, 189 Another group of Meccans sent for Mohammed to see if they could negotiate away this painful division of the tribes. They went over old ground and again Mohammed refused the money and power that was offered. He said they were the ones who needed to decide whether they wanted to suffer in the next world and he had the only solution. If they rejected him and his message, Allah would tend to them. The Quraysh wanted miracles as a proof.

One of the Quraysh said, "Well, if you speak for and represent the only true god, then perhaps Allah could do something for us."

"This land is dry. Let Allah send a river to Mecca."

"We are cramped being next to the mountains. Let Allah open up some space by moving the mountains back."

"Our best members are dead. Let your Allah renew them to life and in particular send back the best leader of our tribe, Qusayy. We will ask Qusayy whether or not you speak truly."

Ishaq189 Mohammed said that he was sent as a messenger, not to do such work. They could either accept his message or reject it and be subject to the loss. Then one of them said, "If you won't use your Allah to help us, then let your Allah help you. Send an angel to confirm you and prove to us that we are wrong. As long as the angel is present, let him make a garden and a fine home for you, and present you with all the gold and silver you need. If you do this, we will know that you represent Allah and we are wrong."

Ishaq189 Mohammed did not perform miracles, because such things were not what Allah had appointed him to do.

Ishaq189 Then one of the Quraysh said, "Then let the heavens be dropped on us in pieces as you say your Lord could do. If you do not we will not believe." Mohammed said that Allah could do that if Allah wished or he might not if he wished.

Ishaq189 They then said, "Did not your Lord know that we would ask you these questions? Then your Lord could have prepared you with better answers. And your Lord could have told you what to tell us if we don't believe. We hear that you are getting this Koran from a man named Al Rahman from another town. We don't believe in Al Rahman. Our conscience is clear. We must either destroy you or you must destroy us. Bring us your angels and we will believe them."

Ishaq191 Mohammed would come to the Kabah and tell the Meccans what terrible punishments that Allah had delivered to the others in history who had not believed their prophets. That was now one of his constant themes: "Allah destroyed others like you who did not listen to men like me."

Ishaq191 One of the Quraysh, Al Nadr, had been to Persia and had learned many tales and sagas from the storytellers there. The traveler would announce, "I can tell a better tale than Mohammed." Then he would proceed to tell them ancient sagas and stories of Persia. "In what way is Mohammed a better storyteller than me?"

STRUGGLES

Ishaq235 A Meccan met Mohammed and said, "Mohammed, stop cursing our gods or we will start cursing your Allah." So Mohammed stopped cursing the Meccan gods.

Ishaq238 A Meccan took an old bone to Mohammed, crumbled it up and blew the dust towards Mohammed. He asked, "Will your Allah revive this bone?" Mohammed said, "Yes, I do say that. Allah will resurrect this bone and you will die. Then Allah will send you to Hell!"

THE SATANIC VERSES

Mohammed was always thinking of how he could persuade all the Meccans. It came to him that the three gods of the Quraysh could intercede with Allah. Mohammed said, "These are the exalted high flying cranes whose intercession is approved." The Meccans were delighted and happy. When Mohammed led prayers at the Kabah, all the Meccans, Muslim and Kafir, took part. The Quraysh hung about after the combined service and remarked how happy they were. The tribe had been unified in worship, as before Islam.

The Koran then revealed that Mohammed was wrong. Meccan gods could have no part in his religion. Satan had made him say those terrible words about how the other gods could help Allah. The retraction by Mohammed made the relations between Islam and the Meccans far worse than it had ever been.

> Koran22:52 *Never have We sent a prophet or messenger before you whom Satan did not tempt with evil desires, but Allah will bring Satan's temptations to nothing. Allah will affirm His revelations, for He is knowing and wise. He makes Satan's suggestions a temptation for those whose hearts are diseased or for those whose hearts are hardened. Truly, is this is why the Kafirs are in great opposition so that those who have been given knowledge will know that the Koran is the truth from their Lord and so that they may believe in it and humbly submit to Him. Allah will truly guide the believers to the right path.*

The Koran is constant in its admonitions about whom a Muslim should befriend.

> Koran4:144 *Believers! Do not take Kafirs as friends over fellow believers. Would you give Allah a clear reason to punish you?*

> Koran5:57 *Oh, you who believe, do not take those who have received the Scriptures [Jews and Christians] before you, who have scoffed and jested at your religion, or who are Kafirs for your friends. Fear Allah if you are true believers. When you call to prayer, they make it a mockery and a joke. This is because they are a people who do not understand.*

THE NIGHT JOURNEY

Ishaq264 One night as he lay sleeping, Mohammed said that the angel Gabriel woke him and took him to Jerusalem to the site of the Temple. There at the temple were Jesus, Abraham, Moses, and other prophets. Mohammed led them in prayer.

Ishaq266 Mohammed reported that Abraham looked exactly like him. Moses was a ruddy faced man, tall, thin, and with curly hair.

Ishaq266 Jesus was light skinned with reddish complexion and freckles and lank hair. He was of medium height.

Ishaq268 After the prayers in Jerusalem, Gabriel brought a fine ladder. Mohammed and Gabriel climbed the ladder to the gates of heaven.

Ishaq268 All the angels who greeted Mohammed, smiled and wished him well, except for one. Mohammed asked Gabriel who was the unsmiling angel. The unsmiling angel was Malik, the Keeper of Hell. Mohammed asked Gabriel to ask Malik if he would show him Hell. So Malik removed the lid to Hell and flames blazed into the air. Mohammed quickly asked for the lid to be put back on Hell.

Ishaq269 At the lowest level of Paradise, Adam sat with the spirits of men passing in front of him. To one he would say, "A good spirit from a good body." And to another spirit he would say, "An evil spirit from an evil body."

Ishaq270 Then Mohammed was taken up to the second level of Paradise and saw Jesus.

Ishaq271 When Mohammed got to the seventh level of Paradise his Lord gave him the duty of prayer.

Ishaq272 One day Mohammed stood with the angel, Gabriel, as the Quraysh performed the rituals of their religion. Among them were the leaders who defended their native culture and religion and opposed Mohammed. When the first leader passed by Gabriel, Gabriel threw a leaf in his face and blinded him. Gabriel then caused the second one to get dropsy which killed him. Gabriel caused the third man to develop an infection which killed him. The fourth man was caused later to step on a thorn which killed him. Gabriel killed the last man who dared not to worship Allah with a brain disease.

MOHAMMED'S PROTECTOR AND WIFE BOTH DIE

Ishaq278 Mohammed's protector was his uncle, Abu Talib. Abu Talib had taken the orphan Mohammed into his home and raised him. He took Mohammed on caravan trading missions to Syria and taught him how to be a businessman. Abu Talib was the clan chief who protected Mohammed's life when the rest of Mecca wanted to harm him. Abu Talib was Mohammed's life and security, but he was damned to Hell, he was not a Muslim and no amount of friendship could prevent that.

After Abu Talib's death, the pressure on Mohammed was greater. It reached the point where one of the Quraysh threw dust at Mohammed. This was the worst that happened in Mecca.

Not long after Abu Talib died, Mohammed's wife Khadija also died. She had been a stalwart supporter of Mohammed throughout their marriage, his chief confidant, the first to convert to Islam, and the mother of his children. Although her death had no political effect, it was an emotional blow to Mohammed.

MARRIAGE

About three months after the death of Khadija, Mohammed married Sauda, a widow and a Muslim.

Abu Bakr[1] had a daughter, Aisha, who was six years old. One night Mohammed dreamed that an angel came to him with a child wrapped in a silk cloth and said "This is your wife." When the cloth was raised, he saw Aisha. He had the dream three times, and decided it was a message from Allah. Shortly after marrying Sauda, Mohammed became betrothed to little Aisha. She would become his favorite wife, although the marriage was not consummated until Aisha was nine years old.

THE BEGINNING OF POWER AND JIHAD IN MEDINA

Medina was about a ten-day journey from Mecca, but since ancient times the Medinans had come to Mecca for the fairs. Medina was half Jewish and half Arabian, and there was an ongoing tension between the two. The Jews worked as farmers and craftsmen and were literate. They were the wealthy class, but their power was slowly waning. In times past the Arabs had raided and stolen from the Jews who retaliated by saying that one day a prophet would come and lead them to victory over the Arabs. In spite of the tensions, the Arab tribe of Khazraj were allied with them.

Ishaq286 So when the members of the Khazraj met Mohammed, they said among themselves, "This is the prophet the Jews spoke of. Let us join ranks with him before the Jews do." They became Muslims, and their tribe was rancorous and divided. They hoped that Islam could unite them, and soon every house in Medina had heard of Islam.

Ishaq289 The next year when the Medinan Muslims returned to Mecca, they took an oath to Mohammed. They returned to Medina, and soon many of Medinans submitted to Islam.

Ishaq294 At the next fair in Mecca, many of the new Muslims from Medina showed up. During the early part of the night about seventy of them left the caravan to meet with Mohammed. He recited the Koran and said, "I invite your allegiance on the basis that you protect me as you would your children." [Now that he had made an oath with the Medinans, he would have to leave Mecca. The Medinans had now severed their ties to their previous allied, the Jews of Medina.] Mohammed smiled and said, "No, blood is blood, and blood not to be paid for is blood not to be paid for." Blood revenge and its obligation were common to both parties. "I will war against them that war against you and be at peace with those at peace with you."

Ishaq299 They asked what they would receive for their oath, Mohammed promised them Paradise. They all shook hands on the deal.

---

1. Abu Bakr was Mohammed's closest companion.

Ishaq313 Up to now, the main tension in the division of the Quraysh tribe over the new religion had been resolved by words. Curses and insults had been exchanged. Mohammed condemned the ancient religion and customs on an almost daily basis. The Quraysh had mocked Mohammed and abused his poorer converts. What blood had been drawn had been in the equivalent of a brawl. Dust had been thrown, but no real violence occurred. No one had died.

POLITICAL POWER

Ishaq336-337 In Medina, Mohammed set to work building the first mosque. There were now two groups of Muslims in Medina, the Quraysh Immigrants from Mecca and the Ansars of Medina — Medinan Muslims who became known as the Helpers.

THE COVENANT

Mohammed wrote up a charter or covenant for a basis of law and government. The religion of Islam now had a political system, and Islam had power over those outside the mosque. All Muslims, whether from Mecca, Medina or elsewhere, were part of a community, *umma,* that excluded others. There was one set of ethics for the Muslims and another set for the Kafirs. Duality was established as a fundamental principle of Islamic ethics.

Ishaq341 Muslims were instructed to oppose any who would sow discord among other Muslims. Muslims should not kill other Muslims, nor side with a Kafir against a Muslim. Muslims were to be friends to each other, to the exclusion of Kafirs. If the blood of a Muslim were shed in jihad, it was to be avenged by another Muslim. Non-believers were not to intervene against Muslims.

MARRIAGE

About seven months after arriving in Medina Mohammed, age fifty-three, consummated his marriage with Aisha, now age nine. She moved out of her father's house into what was to become a compound of apartments adjoining the mosque. She was allowed to bring her dolls into the harem due to her age.

He later married ten other women. [The exact number is in question, 10 is the most probable.}

JIHAD, WAR AGAINST ALL

In a nine year period Mohammed personally attended 27 raids. There were 38 other battles and expeditions. This is a total of 65 armed events, not including assassinations and executions, for an average of one violent event every six weeks. He died without an enemy left standing.

[Chapter 3, Jihad, gives a summary of some of those battles, raids, executions, assassinations and other violent events in Mohammed's life.]

MECCA CONQUERED

Ishaq813-4 The chief of the Meccans, Abu Sufyan, came to the Muslim camp to negotiate. Abu Sufyan went ahead and announced to Mecca that Mohammed's army was coming. They were not to resist but to go into their houses, his house or the Kabah and that they would be safe.

Ishaq819 Mohammed had told his commanders only to kill those who resisted. Otherwise they were to bother no one except for those who had spoken against Mohammed. The list of those to be killed:

- One of Mohammed's secretaries, who had said that when he was recording Mohammed's Koranic revelations sometimes Mohammed let the secretary insert better speech. This caused him to lose faith and he became an apostate (left Islam).
- Two singing girls who had sung satires against Mohammed.
- A Muslim tax collector who had become an apostate (left Islam).
- A man who had insulted Mohammed.

Ishaq821 Mohammed went to the Kabah and rode around it seven times. Each time he went past the Black Stone, he touched it with his stick. Then he called for the key to the Kabah and entered. There was a carved wooden dove that he picked up and broke and threw out the door. Mohammed had all the religious art destroyed.

SUCCESS BRINGS MORE SUCCESS

Ishaq933 The Arabs were waiting to see what would happen between the Quraysh and Mohammed. After Mohammed had taken Mecca and won the battle at Tabuk, deputations began to come from the Arabs. When Mohammed was victorious, the Arabs came in groups and joined with him.

Ishaq956 The kings of Himyar wrote to Mohammed that they had submitted to Islam. Mohammed wrote them back, "... I received your message and am informed of your acceptance of Islam and your killing of

Kafirs. Allah has guided you. ... send one-fifth of the spoils of war and tax the believers... Christians and Jews who do not convert must pay the poll tax..."

Ishaq965 Mohammed sent out tax collectors to every part of Islam to collect the tax.

MOHAMMED'S LAST YEAR

THE FAREWELL PILGRIMAGE

Ishaq968 Ten years after entering Medina, Mohammed made what was to be his last pilgrimage to Mecca. There he made his farewell address. He told the Muslims that usury was abolished, Allah would judge them and their works. All of the blood shed before Islam was to be left unavenged. The lunar calendar was the sacred calendar and it was not to be adjusted with respect to the solar calendar. He defined other rules:

Ishaq969 Men have rights over their wives and wives have rights over their husbands. The wives must never commit adultery nor act in a provocative manner towards others. If they do, they should be put in put in separate rooms and beaten lightly. If they refrain from these things, they have the right to food and clothing. Injunctions should be laid on women lightly for they are prisoners of the men and have no control over their persons.

M473 Muslims were to feed and clothe their slaves well.

Ishaq969 Every Muslim is a Muslim's brother. Muslims were only to take from a brother what he gave freely.

Ishaq970 Mohammed led the Muslims through the rituals of the pilgrimage.

MOHAMMED'S DEATH

Ishaq1006 Mohammed weakened and was in a great deal of pain. Later he died with his head in Aisha's lap. His final words were the perfect summation of Islam, political action based upon religion.

Bukhari4,52,288 *Mohammed said, "There should not be any other religions than Islam in Arabia" and that money should continue to be paid to influence the foreign, Kafir ambassadors.*

Mohammed was buried beneath his bed. The bed was removed and a grave was dug where the bed had stood.

THE HADITH

INTRODUCTION TO THE HADITH

A hadith, or tradition—usually only a paragraph long—is an action, brief story, or conversation about or by Mohammed. The action can be as elementary as Mohammed's drinking a glass of water or putting on his sandals. A collection of these stories is called the Hadith or Traditions. So the Hadith is a collection of hadiths (the actual plural of hadith is *ahadith*).

The Hadith contains the *Sunna* (the ideal speech or action) of Mohammed, that is, his pronouncements. The actual words or deeds, then, that one should follow, are the Sunna; the story that gave rise to the Sunna is the hadith.

There are many collectors of hadiths, but the two most authoritative collectors were Al-Bukhari, or Bukhari, and Abu Muslim, or Muslim. Most of the hadiths in this book come from Bukhari. From 600,000 hadiths, he took the most reliable 6,720 and recorded them in *Sahih of Al-Bukhari*, also known as *Sahih Bukhari*. Muslim's work is called *Sahih Muslim*.

A few of the hadiths are not about Mohammed but about Ali, Umar, Abu Bakr, and Uthman. These four men were Mohammed's closest companions and became caliphs—absolute religious and political rulers of Islam and the equivalent of religious kings. They are called "the rightly guided caliphs," and their Sunna (words and actions) are also considered ideal Islamic behavior.

All of the hadiths in this work have many duplicates or near duplicates—like multiple witnesses recounting the same event. They blend seamlessly with the Koran and the Sira. They do not contradict any of the Islamic doctrine. They are from the most trusted sources of hadiths—Bukhari and Muslim.

POLITICAL HADITH

Most of these hadiths concern Political Islam, in other words, how Islam treats Kafirs. Many of the hadiths are about religious rituals. Mohammed prayed frequently, and the details of his prayer could be recorded as a hadith. Some acts are ritually unclean, for example, going to the bathroom. After an unclean act, an ablution (ritual cleansing) must be performed so a Muslim can enter a state of ritual purity in order to pray or pick up a Koran, for instance. Many different hadiths of ritual purity were preserved.

Since this book is about Political Islam, few of these ritual purity and prayer hadiths are found here, but some of them have been included because they are interesting. We know more about Mohammed's personal habits than those of any other man in history. How he put on his shoes or relieved himself is a model for all humanity for all times.

Lastly, these hadiths are the very foundation of the Sharia, Islamic law. Furthermore, there is no Islam without politics, so the lesson of the Hadith, the Sira, and the Koran is that Islam must rule all politics. The belief is that, since Islamic politics come straight from the only god, it is only a matter of time before Political Islam prevails over all.

These hadiths are sacred literature. All Muslims are to copy the divine pattern of Mohammed's actions and words to be acceptable to the only god, Allah. For Islam, Mohammed is the model political leader, husband, warrior, philosopher, religious leader, and neighbor. Mohammed is the ideal pattern of man for all times and all places.

INTERESTING HADITH

BEHEADING

There are many references to beheadings in both the Sira and the Hadith. Many refer to the beheading of the Jews in Medina, the last of the three Medinan Jewish tribes.

Eight hundred male Jews were beheaded as Mohammed watched with his twelve-year-old wife, Aisha.

Bukhari5,58,148 When some of the remaining Jews of Medina agreed to obey a verdict from Saed, Mohammed sent for him. He approached the Mosque riding a donkey and Mohammed said, "Stand up for your leader." Mohammed then said, "Saed, give these people your verdict." Saed replied, "Their soldiers should be beheaded and their women and children should become slaves." Mohammed, pleased with the verdict, said, "You have made a ruling that Allah or a king would approve of."

JIHAD

The following hadith summarizes all the key elements of jihad. (Only the fourth item, the Day of Resurrection, is purely religious in nature). It tells us that the whole world must submit to Islam; Kafirs are the enemy simply because they are not Muslims. To achieve this dominance Islam may use terror and violence. It may use psychological warfare, fear, theft. It may take the spoils of war from Kafirs. Violence and terror are made sacred by the Koran. Peace comes only with submission to Islam.

Bukhari11,7,331 Mohammed:

I have been given five things which were not given to any one else before me:

1. Allah made me victorious by awe, by His frightening my enemies for a distance of one month's journey.

2. The earth has been made for me and for my followers, a place for praying and a place to perform rituals; therefore, anyone of my followers can pray wherever the time of a prayer is due.

3. The spoils of war has been made lawful for me yet it was not lawful for anyone else before me.

4. I have been given the right of intercession on the Day of Resurrection.

5. Every Prophet used to be sent to his nation only but I have been sent to all mankind.

To be a real Muslim, one must aspire to be a jihadist.

M020,4696 Mohammed: "The man who dies without participating in jihad, who never desired to wage holy war, dies the death of a hypocrite."

Fighting in jihad is demanded for all Muslims except for the frail or the crippled. To sit at home is inferior to jihad. Jihad is an obligation for all times and all places and for all Muslims.

Bukhari6,60,118 After the following verse was revealed to Mohammed, he called for a scribe,

> "Not equal are those believers who sit at home and those who strive and fight in the Cause of Allah."

After the scribe arrived with his writing utensils, Mohammed dictated his revelation. Ibn Um Maktum, who was present, exclaimed, "O Mohammed! But I am blind." A new revelation was then revealed that said:

> Koran4:95 *Believers who stay at home in safety, other than those who are disabled, are not equal to those who fight with their wealth and their lives for Allah's cause [jihad].*

Allah rewards those who give to jihad and curses those who do not.

Bukhari2,24,522 Mohammed: "Two angels descend from Paradise each day. One says, 'O, Allah! Reward those who contribute to jihad,' and the other says, 'O, Allah! Kill those who refuse to support jihad.'"

A jihadist will never go to Hell.

Bukhari4,52,66 Mohammed: "Anyone who gets his feet dirty while participating in jihad will not go to Hell."

APOSTATES

No punishment is too great for the apostate (one who leaves Islam).

Bukhari8,82,797 Some people came to Medina and soon became ill, so Mohammed sent them to the place where the camels were sheltered and told them to drink camel urine and milk as a remedy. They followed his advice, but when they recovered, they killed the shepherd guarding the camels and stole the herd.

In the morning, Mohammed heard what the men had done and ordered their capture. Before noon, the men were captured and brought before Mohammed. He ordered that their hands and feet be cut off and their eyes gouged out with hot pokers. They were then thrown on jagged rocks, their pleas for water ignored and they died of thirst.

Abu said, "They were thieves and murderers who abandoned Islam and reverted to paganism, thus attacking Allah and Mohammed."

When Mohammed died, entire tribes wanted to leave Islam. The first wars fought by Islam were against these apostates, and thousands were killed.

The apostasy wars were fought after Mohammed died. Here we see that taxes were also a reason to kill apostates (apostates won't pay taxes).

Bukhari2,23,483 After the death of Mohammed, Abu Bakr became the caliph, and he declared war against a group of Arabs who reverted back to paganism.

Umar asked Abu Bakr, "How can you war against these men when you remember that Mohammed said, 'I have been ordered by Allah to continue the fight until all the people say, "There is no god except Allah," and whoever says this will have his life and possessions protected from my anger. The exceptions being legal regulations that are adjudicated by man; Allah will settle all accounts.

Abu Bakr said, "I will fight those who argue that no difference exists between the tax [the poor tax was a Muslim obligation] and the prayer.

The tax is an obligation put upon man by Allah. If someone should refuse to pay me even the smallest amount that they used to pay during the time of Mohammed, then I will fight them for doing so."

Umar then said, "Allah spoke to Abu Bakr, and I now know that he was right."

Bukhari9,83,17 Mohammed: "A Muslim who has admitted that there is no god but Allah and that I am His prophet may not be killed except for three reasons: as punishment for murder, for adultery, or for reverting back to non-belief after accepting Islam."

MOHAMMED

Bukhari1,3,63 We were sitting with Mohammed in the Mosque one day when a man rode up on a camel. He asked, "Which one of you is Mohammed?" We answered, "That white man leaning on his arm…"

Bukhari7,65,292 Mohammed preferred to begin things from the right side; combing his hair, putting on his shoes, or performing ablution. He would follow this practice in every thing he did.

M023,5018 Anas said that Mohammed forbade people to drink while standing. Qatada related: We asked him, "What about eating while standing?" Anas said, "That is even more objectionable."

M023,5029 Anas related the story that Mohammed would drink his refreshments in three gulps.

Bukhari7,72,807 One day a man peeped into Mohammed's house and saw him scratching his head with a comb. Noticing the man Mohammed said, "If I had realized that you were peeking at me I would have stuck this comb in your eye. The reason that people must ask permission is to keep them from seeing things that they shouldn't."

Mohammed had a temper.

Bukhari8,73,130 There was once a curtain with pictures of animals on it in my [Aisha's] house. When Mohammed saw it, his face became flushed with anger. He tore it to bits and said, "People that paint such pictures will receive Hell's most terrible punishment on Judgment Day."

MAGIC

Bukhari4,53,400 A spell was put on Mohammed one time that caused him to believe he had laid with his wives and he had not. He spent a long time praying to Allah and finally came to us and said, "Allah has shown me how break the spell."

I saw two people in a dream. One sat at my head and the other sat at my feet. The first man asked the other, "What is wrong with this man?" The second man said, "He is under a bewitching spell." The first man asked, "Who has cast the spell?" The second man answered, "Lubaid." "What did he use?" the first asked. The other man replied, "A comb with hair on it, and the pollen from a date palm." The first man then asked, "Where is it kept?" He was told, "In the Dharwan well."

Mohammed visited the well, and upon his return he told me that "the date palm trees near the well look like devil's heads." I asked if he had removed the charm that was used to bewitch him from the well, and he said that he had not. "No, Allah cured me. I don't want the people to be tempted to evil." Some time later the well was filled with earth.

EVIL EYE

Bukhari4,55,590 Mohammed would beseech Allah to protect Al-Hasan and Al-Husain. He would say, "Our ancestor, Abraham, would beseech Allah to protect Ishmael and Isaac by saying, "Allah, the Koran protects me from all venomous creatures and every evil eye.'"

Bukhari7,71,636 Mohammed said, "There is no disputing the existence of an evil eye." He also forbade tattooing.

SATAN

M023,5046 Mohammed: "Satan is with you in everything that you do. He is there when you are eating, therefore if you drop any food from your mouth, you should brush away any dirt and eat it. Do not leave any for Satan. When you finish eating, lick your fingers clean, because you do not know where the blessing resides in the food."

Bukhari2,21,243 Mohammed: "Satan puts three knots on the back of a sleeping persons head. On each knot he imprints these words, 'Stay asleep; the night is long.' When a person wakes up and thinks of Allah, one knot is untied; when a person performs purification, another knot is untied, when a person says his prayers, the third knot is untied and the person awakes with energy and a kind heart. If any knots remain, the person wakes up lazy with a vexing heart."

M024,5279 Mohammed: "The bell is Satan's musical instrument." [Think of church bells.]

Bukhari2,22,301 One time after giving the daily prayer Mohammed said, "Satan faced me and attempted to disrupt my prayer, but Allah gave me strength and I strangled him. I considered tying him to a pillar in the mosque so that the people could see him in the morning. However, I recalled the words of Solomon, 'Lord, give me a kingdom the like of which will belong to no other.' Allah then forced Satan to return from where he came with his head bent low with shame."

Bukhari4,54,492 Someone mentioned to Mohammed a man that slept long after sunrise. Mohammed said, "Satan has urinated in that man's ears."

Bukhari4,54,500 Mohammed: "At dusk, keep your children near, because the devil is out. After an hour they may roam. Invoke Allah's name and close your house gates at night. Invoke Allah's name and cover your dishes. If your dishes lack covers, then place some wood or something over them."

Bukhari4,54,506 Mohammed: "When a person is born, Satan touches him with two fingers. Jesus, Mary's son, was the exception. Satan tried to touch him, but missed and touched placenta instead."

Bukhari8,73,242 Mohammed: "Allah hates yawning and likes sneezing. The obligatory Muslim response to someone sneezing and giving praise to Allah is to say 'May Allah give you mercy.' Yawning, however, is caused by Satan. Stifle a yawn as soon as possible. If a person says, "Ha," while yawning, Satan will cause him mischief."

Bukhari7,71,643 I [Abu Qatada] was there when Mohammed said, "Allah gives good dreams, bad dreams are from Satan. If any of you experience something unpleasant during a dream, they should seek protection with Allah and blow three times to the left. This will protect you."

JINNS AND SPIRITS

Jinns are nonmaterial creatures who can help and hurt humans. Humans are made from earth and jinns are made from fire. Jinns occur in the Koran as well; one sura is titled "The Jinns."

Bukhari5,58,199 Masruq and I [Abdur-Rahman] were talking and I asked him, "Who told Mohammed about the jinns listening to the Koran?" He replied, "Your father, Abdullah, told me that Mohammed heard about them from a tree."

Bukhari5,58,200 While accompanying Mohammed, I [Abu Huraira] spent some time carrying water for purification and cleaning. One time,

Mohammed asked, "Who are you?" I answered, "Abu Huraira." He said, "Get me some stones so I may wipe myself, and take care that you don't bring me any dried dung or bone."

I carried some stones over to him in the hem of my robe, left them by his side and I walked away. Later I asked him what was the significance of the bone and the dung and he said, "That is what jinns eat."

The jinn delegate from Nasibin—a very charming jinn—asked that they might have the residue from human food. I interceded with Allah for them that they might never be hungry as long as there was dung and bones for them to feed upon.

SCIENCE

Bukhari4,54,421 One day as the sun was setting, Mohammed asked me [Abu Dhar], "Do you know where the sun goes at night?" I said, "You and Allah know better than I." Mohammed said, "It travels until it sits under the throne of Allah where it waits until permission is given to rise. A day will come when the sun will not be allowed to rest, nor continue on its regular path. It will instead be ordered to return the way it came and will rise in the west. That is how I interpret Allah's revelation:

Koran36:37 *The night is a sign for them. We withdraw it from the day and plunge them into darkness, and the sun runs its mandated course.*

Bukhari4,55,549 Mohammed said about human conception, for the first forty days after conception, each of us forms in a mother's womb. The next forty days is spent as a clot of blood, and the next forty as a bit of flesh. Then an angel is sent by Allah to write four determining words that signify a person's destiny: his actions, his time of death, his occupation, and whether he will be blessed or cursed by Allah. A soul is then infused in his body.

CURES

Bukhari7,67,446 Mohammed was asked about a mouse that fell into some butter fat and died. He said to dispose of the mouse and the butter-fat around it, but keep and eat the remaining butter fat."

Bukhari7,71,673 Mohammed: "If a fly drops into a container of liquid, submerge it in the liquid and throw the fly away. In one wing of the fly is a disease, but in the other is a cure for the disease."

Mohammed on disease.

Bukhari7,71,614 A man said to Mohammed, "My brother suffers from diarrhea." Mohammed said, "Tell him to drink honey." The man returned to Mohammed and said, "He drank the honey, but it made his condition worse." Mohammed said, "Allah tells the truth and your brother's stomach tells a lie."

RITUALS OF ELIMINATION

Bukhari1,4,144 When Mohammed went to relieve himself, he would say, "Allah, protect me from evil spirits and from wicked actions."

Bukhari1,8,388 Mohammed said, "Do not face toward or away from Mecca while defecating. Instead face either west or east." Abu Aiyub also said, "Arriving in Sham, we found toilets facing Mecca. So, we used them, but turned our faces sideways and begged Allah to forgive us."

Bukhari1,4,156 Mohammed: "Do not hold yourself or clean yourself with your right hand. When drinking, do not breathe into the cup."

FLATULENCE

Bukhari1,8,436 Mohammed: "As long as a person is properly praying and does not break wind, the angels will continue to ask Allah's forgiveness for you. The angels say, 'Allah be merciful. Forgive him.'"

Bukhari8,73,68 Mohammed outlawed laughing at someone for breaking wind.

SPITTING

Bukhari1,8,404 Mohammed: "Nobody should spit directly in front of himself or to his right, rather he should spit to his left or beneath his foot."

ART

Bukhari7,72,843 Mohammed grew depressed one day after Gabriel's promised visit was delayed. When Gabriel came at last, Mohammed complained about the delay. Gabriel said to him, "Angels will not enter a house that contains a dog or a picture."

A BRIEF HISTORY OF JIHAD

JIHAD

Duality of ethics was the basis for Mohammed's greatest single innovation—jihad. Jihad is dual ethics with sacred violence. The key religious element of the dual ethics is that Allah sanctifies violence for complete domination. The non-Muslims must submit to Islam.

Jihad is usually called "holy war" but this is far too narrow a view. Jihad means struggle or effort and is a process that is shown by the life of Mohammed, the perfect jihadist. In Mecca, Mohammed demonstrated the initial practice of jihad when Islam was weak: persuasion and conversion. When he moved to Medina, he demonstrated how jihad worked when Islam was strong: using immigration against inhabitants, creating political power by struggling against the host, dominating other religions, using violence, and establishing a government.

THE JIHAD OF MECCA

From the standpoint of war, jihad did not begin until Mohammed's first killing attack in Medina. But its roots go back to Mecca when Mohammed cursed the ancient native Arabic gods. Jihad is a force that still manifests itself according to circumstances. The violence may go no further than aggressive arguments, beatings, put-downs, hostility, insults, or threats, but it is always based upon an ethical system of duality that started in Mecca.

In Mecca, Mohammed promised his critics' slaughter. When heated arguments broke out between the Meccans and Muslims, it was a Muslim who picked up a weapon and drew blood. It was a Muslim, Umar, who violently protested over a poem. Mohammed was in Mecca when he signed a blood oath with the Muslims of Medina.

The root of the violence of Medina was the peace of Mecca. A peace that demanded submission.

ARABIC JIHAD

Mohammed fought for the last nine years of his life. Near the end he sent letters to the surrounding kingdoms demanding that they submit to Islam. Islam demands that all jihad be seen as defensive, but we can see that Mohammed planned an offence against all the Kafirs.

Umar was the second caliph. He sent his armies against the Persian Empire. The Hadith records his reasons for jihad.

> Bukhari 4,53,386 *So, Umar sent us to Persia. When we reached the land of the enemy, the representative of the Persians came out with forty-thousand warriors, and an interpreter got up saying, "Let one of you talk to me!"*
>
> *[...] Our Prophet, the Messenger of our Lord, has ordered us to fight you till you worship Allah alone or give jizya (i.e. tribute); and our Prophet has informed us that our Lord says: "Whoever amongst us is killed (i.e. martyred), shall go to Paradise to lead such a luxurious life as he has never seen, and whoever amongst us remain alive, shall become your master."*

The situation was ripe for plunder. The Persians and the Byzantines (Christians) had fought until exhaustion. Jihad captured the Jerusalem, Persia, Egypt, North Africa and the Middle East. Islam became wealthy off of the plunder. It was a catastrophe for Christianity.

What is remarkable is the Christian response. They did not ever refer to Islam, but Arabs. They saw the invasion as punishment for other Christians' wrong doctrine and their own sins. They quoted Revelation and Daniel. They were even gleeful when Islam crushed other Christians who differed in doctrine (heretics). They deserved it and they saw Islam as being divinely driven. Except, of course, when it came their turn.

Church buildings were desecrated, treasure taken, farmland ruined, cities were destroyed. It was a reign of terror. But it was not just money; it was a civilization that was annihilated. If an Egyptian Copt (the original Egyptians, the sons of the pharaohs) spoke Coptic in front of a Muslim official, his tongue was cut out. Is it any wonder that Arabic became the language of Egypt? Is it any wonder that when Napoleon arrived 1100 years later, no Egyptian could tell him what the pyramids were about?

This became true of every nation. Civilizations vanished like dinosaurs to be replaced by Islamic civilization. Saint Augustine was from Algeria, a European civilization. (North Africa was part of Europe, the Roman Empire). There is not one church in North Africa today. This is fate of all civilizations under Islam.

Here is Michael the Syrian's account of the Muslim invasion of Cappodocia (southern Turkey) in 650 AD under Caliph Umar:

> ... when Muawiya [the Muslim commander] arrived [in Euchaita in Armenia] he ordered all the inhabitants to be put to the sword; he placed guards so that no one escaped. After gathering up all the wealth of the town, they set to torturing the leaders to make them show them things [treasures] that had been hidden. The Taiyaye [Muslim Arabs] led everyone into slavery -- men and women, boys and girls -- and they committed much debauchery in that unfortunate town: they wickedly committed immoralities inside churches. They returned to their country rejoicing[1].

SPAIN

Once North African Christianity was crushed, Islam turned to Christian Spain.

The following description by the Muslim historian, Ibn al-Athir (1160-1233 AD), of razzias (raiding expeditions) in Northern Spain and France in the eighth and ninth centuries AD, conveys nothing but satisfaction at the extent of the destruction wrought upon the infidels, including noncombatants.

> In 793 AD, Hisham, prince of Spain, sent a large army commanded by Abd al-Malik b. Abd al-Wahid b. Mugith into enemy territory, and which made forays as far as Narbonne and Jaranda . This general first attacked Jaranda where there was an elite Frank garrison; he killed the bravest, destroyed the walls and towers of the town and almost managed to seize it. He then marched on to Narbonne, where he repeated the same actions, then, pushing forward, he trampled underfoot the land of the Cerdagne [near Andorra in the Pyrenees]. For several months he traversed this land in every direction, violating women, killing warriors, destroying fortresses, burning and pillaging everything, driving back the enemy who fled in disorder. He returned safe and sound, dragging behind him God alone knows how much booty. This is one of the most famous expeditions of the Muslims in Spain. In 837 AD, Abd ar-Rahman b. al Hakam, sovereign of Spain, sent an army against Alava; it encamped near Hisn al-Gharat, which it besieged; it seized the booty that was found there, killed the inhabitants and withdrew, carrying off women and children as captives. In 845 AD, a Muslim army advanced into Galicia on the territory of the

---

1   *The Decline of Eastern Christianity under Islam*, Bat Ye'or, Associated University Press, 1996, 276-7.

infidels, where it pillaged and massacred everyone. In 860 AD, Muhammad b. Abd ar-Rahman advanced with many troops and a large military apparatus against the region of Pamplona. He reduced, ruined and ravaged this territory, where he pillaged and sowed death[1].

But the Arabic phase of jihad came to an end. They controlled Europe from southern France to India and north into Russia. But the Mongols came out of the steps and crushed Baghdad. It was time for the new Muslims, the Turks to rise to power.

TURKISH JIHAD

The Turks were nomads in west Asia who converted to Islam. Before their conversion they were slave traders who sold slaves to the Arab Muslims of Baghdad. As Arab strength weakened, the hardy Turks rose to power in Islam. They attacked Greek Christianity in what was called Anatolia, Asia Minor. At the battle of Mansikert, 1071, the Christians lost to the Turks. Now the approach to Constantinople was open.

In 1493 one of the greatest tragedies in human history happened. Constantine fell. The violation of women and taking plunder were massive. Now the door to Europe was open.

More than any other people, the Turks love war and pillage. They show it in their relations among themselves, what then is the lot of Christians? [...] The Turks went on foot as far as the Danube in order to subjugate the Christians. They invaded this or that province in their tens of thousands; they came like brigands and fled once they had pillaged it. These raids turned all Thrace as far as Dalmatia into a desert. Even the Albanians, who are an innumerable people, were reduced in number. All in all, the Turks destroyed the Wallachians, the Serbs and the Byzantines. When they subdued these peoples, they gave the fifth part of the booty to their sultan in accordance with their law. In this way, they gave up this fifth share, which is the best, to the authorities. Afterwards, when the representatives of the authorities saw a strong, young prisoner, they purchased him at a ridiculously low price and declared him a slave of the state. The sultan called these orphans, his new troops, *janissaries*.[2]

The janissaries are unknown to most Christians. Christians in the Balkans had to give a son to the Turkish ruler as a tax payment. The Turkish

---

1   *The Decline of Eastern Christianity under Islam*, Bat Ye'or, Associated University Press, 1996 281-2.

2   Ibid, pg. 56

army came and carried off the son, who was raised as a Muslim and became an elite soldier for the sultan. Of course, the janissaries were used against Christians. Christian sons were used for jihad against Christianity. Islam has the most brilliant approach to war ever seen in human history.

Turkey was the springboard to attack the Christian Eastern Europe. At Kosovo the Turks beat the combined Christian armies lead by the Serbian king, St. Lazar. The Christian Serbs of today still remember how their ancestors were crushed at Kosovo. Today NATO and the US are on the side of Islam in Eastern Europe. Why? Because we don't have any idea of what has happened in Eastern Europe? We have no sense of history.

Christian Europe recorded the annihilation as a Turkish invasion, not Islamic jihad. They were never to understand Islam and jihad. They saw the Turks as just another political power to be watched and placated. Europe then and now believes that Islam can be dealt with as an ordinary power.

The high point of the Islamic invasion of Europe was reached on September 11, 1868. Islam was driven back from the gates of Vienna. But in 2001, September 11, Islam settled that score. But the US had not one clue as to the significance of the date. We don't remember history. We just repeat our ignorance of Islamic history.

MODERN JIHAD

Islam entered a decline. In 1856 the Europeans made the Turks abolish the formal status of dhimmi for the Christians. But being forced to treat Christians as humans did not go well for the Muslims. However, Islam's memory never forgets a wrong or a loss. In 1876 the Turks slaughtered 30,000 Bulgarians for resisting Islamic government by trying to revolt against Turkish rule.

Then in 1896 the Turks started on the Armenian Christians with the killing of 250,000. Then in 1915, the Turks killed 1,500,000 Armenians in jihad.

Here are the jihadists' marching orders from the leading Turkish Islamic leader:

"Oh Moslems," the document read, "Ye who are smitten with happiness and are on the verge of sacrificing your life and your good for the cause of right, and of braving perils, gather now around the Imperial throne." ... "The deeds of our enemies have brought down the wrath of God. A gleam of hope has appeared. All Mohammedans, young and old, men, women, and children must fulfill their duty. ... If we do it, the deliverance of the

29

subjected Mohammedan kingdoms is assured." ... "He who kills even one unbeliever," one pamphlet read, "of those who rule over us, whether he does it secretly or openly, shall be rewarded by God."[1]

Then in 1922 the Turks murdered 150,000 Christians in Smyrna under the eyes of the West.

Today we see jihad against us in America, against the Serbs in Kosovo and in Yugoslavia and the Russians in Chechnya. In India, Hinds die on a regular basis. Jihad has been declared against the Buddhists in Thailand. There is no continent that has not had jihad attacks in the 20th century.

These small accounts are part of a 1400 years of suffering of people who had only one failing, they were Christians. 60,000,000 of them.

THE SUPREME MASTER OF COMPLETE WAR

Mohammed was the supreme master of complete war and has had no equal to this day. His understanding of the use of force was sophisticated and subtle. Physical violence was only a small part of his understanding of war. That is why comparisons make him superior to military men such as Julius Caesar. Other military geniuses established empires, but none of them had a process for war and empire that lasted for fourteen-hundred years and is still going strong.

Mohammed's profound insight was not just the waging of physical war but war of the mind, emotions, culture, politics, and religion. There is no aspect of being human that Mohammed did not use for war. Money, salvation, culture, religion, destiny, family, immigration, legal codes, government, power, deceit, racial pride, tribalism, community, fear, propaganda, diplomacy, spy-craft, philosophy, ethics, and psychology were all used for jihad. Jihad was not holy war but complete and total civilizational war.

THE SIRA—JIHAD, WAR AGAINST ALL

In Mecca, Mohammed had divided the community into Islam and the separate factions of the native Arabic religions. In Mecca he adopted all the classical Jewish stories to prove his prophesy and spoke well of the Jews. As there were few Jews living in Mecca, there was no one to differ with him.

---

1   *The Burning Tigris*, Peter Balakian, pgs.169-70.)

In Medina half of the population were Jews, who let Mohammed know that they disagreed with him. So in Medina, Mohammed argued with Jews as well as the Kafir Arabs. Even though there were very few in the town who were Christian, Mohammed argued against them as well. All Kafirs were verbally attacked in Medina.

Ishaq415 It was thirteen years after he started preaching and one to two years after going to Medina that Mohammed prepared for war as commanded by Allah. He would fight his enemies, those who were not Muslims.

THE FIRST RAIDS

Ishaq416-423 Mohammed sent forth his fighters on seven armed raids to find the trade caravans headed to Mecca.

JIHAD—THE FIRST KILLING

Ishaq423-4 Mohammed sent Abdullah out with eight men. A caravan of the Quraysh passed by the Muslims as they overlooked the road from a rise. When the Quraysh saw them they were scared because they had slept not too far from here, but one of the Muslims had a shaved head. Since a shaved head was a mark of a pilgrim, the Quraysh felt better. They were safe. They were also in a sacred month when weapons were not carried.

Ishaq425 The Muslims took council. They were in a dilemma. If they attacked the caravan that day, they would be killing in a sacred month. They decided to go ahead with the attack, kill as many as possible, and take their goods.

Ishaq425 Islam drew first blood against the Quraysh of Mecca. They attacked the unarmed men. Amr was killed by an arrow. He was the first man to be killed in jihad. One man escaped and they captured two prisoners. They loaded the camels and headed back to Mohammed in Medina. On the way they talked about how Mohammed would get one-fifth of the stolen goods as the spoils of war.

Ishaq425 When they got back, Mohammed said that he did not order them to attack in the sacred month. So he held the caravan and the two prisoners in suspense and refused to do anything with the goods or prisoners. The prisoners said, "Mohammed has violated the sacred month, shed blood therein, stolen goods and taken prisoners."

Ishaq426 The Koran replied that the Meccans resisted the doctrine of Islam and tried to persuade Muslims to drop their faith was worse than killing. Before Islam, the rule of justice in Arabia was a killing for a killing,

31

but now to resist Islam was worse than murder. Those who argue against Islam and resist Islam can be killed as a sacred act. The spoils were distributed and a ransom set for the prisoners. The men who had killed and stolen were now concerned as to whether they would get their take of the spoils. So the Koran revealed that as Muslims who had been exiled and fought, they were blessed by Allah. They received their share and Mohammed took his one-fifth of the spoils of war.

COMMENT

The promised violence of Mecca bore fruit. Jihad is the full fruition of the dualistic ethics.

The first successful jihad was a prototype:

- The attempts were untiring, it took seven failed tries to get to success.
- It was a sneak attack.
- It had an economic target.
- A religious disguise was used. Deception was a key element. Religion was a shield for political action.
- Kafir death was approved by the Koran.
- Theft from the Kafir was sanctioned as a moral act.
- There were clearly two sets of ethics. One for Islam and one for the Kafirs.
- It was a defensive attack. The Kafirs' resistance to Islam violates sacred law and was an offense against Allah.
- Muslims may settle Allah's accounts.

THE SIRA—THE BATTLE OF BADR

Ishaq428 Mohammed heard that Abu Sufyan was coming with a large caravan of thirty to forty Quraysh from Syria. Mohammed called the Muslims together and said, "Go out and attack it, perhaps Allah will give us the prey."

Ishaq433 Mohammed and his men headed out of Medina for what would prove to be one of the most important battles in all of history, a battle that would change the world forever.

Ishaq435 Mohammed was cheered. He said, "I see the enemy dead on the ground." They headed towards Badr and camped near there for the night.

Before Islam, killing of kin and tribal brothers had been forbidden since the dawn of time. After Islam was established, brother would kill

32

brother and sons would kill their fathers, fighting in Allah's cause—jihad. Mohammed would change all the rules of war in Arabia and the world.

Ishaq456 Islam won against an army three times its size. Then it was time to take the property from the dead was now the spoils of jihad and the profit of Islam. Mohammed divided it equally among all who were there. He took one-fifth for himself.

Ishaq477 The Muslims were not alone. No, Allah sent a thousand angels to help kill those who worshiped in the ancient ways and rituals. To resist Mohammed was a death sentence from Allah. When a Muslim meets a Kafir in war, he should never turn his back, except as a tactical maneuver. A Muslim fighting in Allah's cause must face the enemy. To not do so brings on the wrath of Allah and the judgment of Hell.

Mohammed left Mecca as a preacher and prophet. He entered Medina with about 150 Muslim converts. After a year in Medina there were about 250-300 Muslims and most of them were very poor. After the battle of Badr, a new Islam emerged. Mohammed rode out of Medina as a politician and general. Islam became an armed political force with a religious motivation, jihad.

COMMENTS

In dealing with Kafirs, there are no moral limits. Torture is a tactic of war. Allah tortures the Kafirs in the afterlife, so a Muslim can use torture in jihad in this life.

Killing the Kafir pleases Allah; so killing is a pleasure and is to be done without mercy and with joy. There is never any regret or sadness at killing. Killing the Kafir is a normal activity. [But dualism allows for the same Muslim to be a good neighbor.]

No slight against Islam is forgotten. Any resistance to Islam may be punished by death. To kill the Kafirs who oppose Islam is to merely turn the Kafir over to Allah for eternal torture.

Jihad is political and prepares the way for the end of Kafir civilization.

Allah praises those who kill without the thought of their own death. To be afraid in jihad is a form of blasphemy. The highest form of morality is to die while trying to destroy the civilization of the Kafir for the advancement of Islam.

The leader of jihad submits to Islam and his followers are to obey his every command.

Jihad uses the momentum of victory to move to the next attack. Jihad is relentless.

Beheading is an Islamic technique of killing and is pure Sunna.

THE SIRA—JIHAD, A SETBACK

THE BATTLE OF UHUD

Ishaq555 With their army in defeat after the battle of Badr, and their best men slain, the Meccans went to the Quraysh elders and requested money, arms and more men to launch a counterattack to defeat the despised Mohammed. The city raised the money and a new army bent on revenge was formed.

Ishaq558 The Meccan army set out for Medina, set up camp near the city and prepared for war.

Ishaq560 Mohammed had a thousand troops at his disposal, and warned them not to begin fighting until he gave the word. The area where the battle was to be fought was in a valley. Mohammed positioned his army with Mt. Uhud to its rear. There was, however, the possibility that the Meccans could send troops through a vulnerable opening in the mountain and attack Mohammed's forces from the rear. To prevent this, Mohammed stationed a force of fifty archers on a hill above his left flank in order to protect the main force. He instructed them not to move until the battle was over, whether the Muslims won or not.

Ishaq570 The Muslims fought valiantly and quickly cut the Meccans off from their camp. Seeing that they were in danger of defeat, the Meccan army dropped their arms and equipment and began to flee back behind the lines. As the archers poured down onto the battlefield to retrieve war booty, a group of Meccan warriors, who had made their way around the mountain and taken up a position behind Mohammed, launched their attack. The remaining archers were killed and the battle suddenly went against the Muslims.

Ishaq571 They retreated and many were slain. Mohammed himself sustained facial cuts and a broken tooth.

Ishaq583 The day went to the Meccans, the Quraysh. The Meccans did not press their advantage. They came to extract tribal justice but they did not want to dominate Islam. Abu Sufyan, the Meccan leader, agreed through an emissary that they would meet again the following year.

The Meccans' mind of war was tribal. The Islamic mind of war was about annihilation of the Kafir culture and not about the old war traditions of "fighting fair".

ASSASSINATION AS JIHAD

M276 After Uhud, several tribes allied themselves under the leadership of Sufyan Ibn Khalid. Mohammed dispatched an assassin to kill him, for without his leadership the coalition would fall apart. So the assassin, Abdullah, joined his forces and waited until he was alone with him. He killed Sufyan and cut off his head and went straight to Mohammed. Mohammed welcomed him and asked him how it had gone. Abdullah presented Mohammed with the head of his enemy. Mohammed was gratified and presented him with his walking stick. He said, "This is a token between you and me on the day of resurrection. Very few will have such to lean on in that day." Abdullah attached it to his sword scabbard.

COMMENTS

The battle of Uhud gave Islam a necessary element of the mind of war—the ability to maintain morale in the face of defeat. A defeat is only a sign of not being a good enough Muslim. Doubt is a sin.

The mental position of the jihadists is that what they do is not personal. It is all for Allah. The jihadists should have no thought for themselves. In particular, they should never have any fear or doubt.

The Kafirs tried to play by the old tribal rules, not realizing that this was a civilizational war of annihilation. Getting-even or fair-play limits the mind of war. Islam does not obey such limitations. There are no Geneva Conventions of jihad.

Mohammed's deception about his strength after losing the battle shows that jihad is a mental game of great subtlety. The psychology of war is Islam's great strength. Posturing is an important element of war.

Assassination of the intellectuals who oppose Islam spreads fear so that intellectuals cannot help their civilization.

THE SIRA—MOHAMMED'S FINAL JIHAD

THE RAID ON MUTA

Ishaq791-3 Mohammed sent an army of 3,000 to Muta soon after his return from Mecca. Now Muta was north of Medina, near Syria. When they arrived the Muslims found a large army of the Byzantines [Greek Christians] waiting. They argued about what to do. One of them said, "Men, you are complaining of what you came here to do. Die as martyrs. Islam does not fight with numbers or strength but with Islam. Come! We have only two prospects. Victory or martyrdom, both are fine. Let us go forward!"

Ishaq796 The Muslims were cut to ribbons because the Byzantines were professionals and were superior in numbers.

THE BATTLE OF HUNAIN

Ishaq840 When Mohammed took Mecca, the surrounding Arab tribes realized that if he was not opposed he would be King of Arabia. The Hawazin Arabs decided to oppose him under the leadership of Malik.

Ishaq842 Mohammed sent a spy to gather intelligence about the Arabs. When he received the information, he began planning for jihad.

Ishaq845 When the army descended into the broad area chosen for the battle, they found the enemy prepared and hiding, waiting to attack. The Muslim troops broke and ran. Mohammed stood in his stirrups and called out, "Where are you going? Come to me, the Apostle of Allah." Most of the men continued to retreat except his battle-hardened core troops who regrouped around him. A core of a hundred men lead the charge to turn the tide. They were steadfast. Mohammed looked at the carnage and said, "Now the oven is hot!" Islam won again.

THE RAID ON TABUK

Ishaq894 Mohammed decided to raid the Byzantine Christians. Normally he never let his men actually know where he was headed. He would announce a destination, but after they were on the way, he would reveal the actual place. This raid was far away in very hot weather, so greater preparations had to be made.

Ishaq902 When they got to Tabuk, the people there paid the poll tax, *jizya*. By paying the poll tax, a per person tax, they would not be attacked, killed or robbed by the Muslims. Those who paid the jizya were under the protection of Islam

Ishaq903 Mohammed sent Khalid to the fort of a Christian chief. When the chief and his brother rode out of their fort to inspect the cattle, Khalid killed the chief's brother and captured the ruler. The chief agreed to pay the poll tax to Islam. Mohammed returned to Medina.

ETERNAL JIHAD

M448 After all the victories, some Muslims said that the days of fighting were over and even began to sell their arms. But Mohammed forbid this, saying, "There shall not cease from the midst of my people a party engaged in fighting for the truth, until the Antichrist appears." Jihad was recognized as the normal state of affairs.

COMMENTS

The raid on Muta was the first to show how Islam was to become a global power.

Mohammed's conquest of Mecca showed he had no tolerance for any criticism. His first political move was to kill all artists and intellectuals who opposed Islam. There is no such thing as an honest disagreement with Islam. He then destroyed all the religious art. Every aspect of a civilization must become Islamic—art, literature, entertainment, law, history, names, customs, food, dress, language, education and so on.

Jihad is eternal; it will cease when the last Kafir is annihilated or submits to Islam.

Every Muslim is to contribute to charities that fund jihad. Those who do not support jihad are hypocrites.

In Islam the mind of war is at a constant readiness. War is the natural state. A Muslim pacifist is a hypocrite.

Dhimmitude of the Christians and Jews was marked by the special tax, the *jizya*, the dhimmi tax. The tax rate can be 50%.

THE JEWS

In Islam's early days, Mohammed began to preach in Mecca where there were a few Jews and a handful of Christians. Mohammed claimed to be the last in the line of Jewish prophets. The stories in the Koran resembled the Jews' stories of Adam, Moses, Noah, and other figures in Jewish tradition. The Meccans had a great deal of respect for the Jews because they had a sacred text. Indeed, both Jews and Christians were called People of the Book. None of the Arabian religions had a religious text, as the native Arabic religions were tribal and based on oral traditions.

Then Mohammed went to Medina. Half of Medina was Jewish. Their leaders did not agree with Mohammed that he was a Jewish prophet. The revelations of the Koran took on a different tone about the Jews. Their scriptures did not agree with Mohammed's, therefore their scriptures were wrong. Clearly they had changed them to oppose Mohammed. Less than two years later, there were no Jews left in Medina, and the Muslims had their possessions.

DEMEANING HADITHS

This is part of a daily prayer by all Muslims.
Bukhari1,12,749 Mohammed: "Say Amen when the Imam says, 'not the path of those who anger You [the Jews] nor the path of those who go astray [the Christians]' everyone who says Amen will have their past sins forgiven."

Bukhari2,23,457 While walking after dark, Mohammed heard a mournful cry and said, "Jews are being punished in the afterlife."

Mohammed claimed the mantle of all the Jewish prophets. He claimed that Allah was Jehovah and that all religious truth came through Allah. Islam has the best claim to Moses.
Bukhari3,31,222 After coming to Medina, Mohammed witnessed the Jews observing a fast on the day of Ashura. Asked about that, they said, "This is a holy day. It celebrates the day God delivered the Jews from their enemy. Moses fasted this day." Mohammed told them, "Muslims have more right to claim Moses as a prophet than you do." Consequently, Mohammed fasted that day and required all Muslims to fast on that day.

Bukhari4,56,662 Mohammed said, "You will imitate the sinful behavior of your ancestors so utterly and completely that if they did something stupid, you would do exactly the same thing."

We asked, "Are you talking about the Jews and the Christians?"

He answered, "Who else could I be talking about but the Jews and the Christians?"

Bukhari4,56,664 Aisha despised the practice of praying with hands on the flanks because that was the way the Jews used to pray.

Bukhari4,56,668 Mohammed: "When the head of a Jew or a Christian becomes gray, they refuse to dye their hair. You must do the opposite of their behavior. Therefore, dye your hair and beard when they become gray."

Jews are the cause of decay and rebellious wives.

Bukhari4,55,547 Mohammed: "If it weren't for the Jews, meat would not rot. If not for Eve, wives would never disobey their mates."

JEWS ARE FALSE; ISLAM IS THE TRUTH

Islam is pure and true. The Jews and their scriptures are corrupt and untrue, and the same is true of Christians and their scripture.

Bukhari3,48,850 Ibn Abbas: "Muslims, why do you ask the Jews or Christians anything? The Koran, revealed directly to Mohammed, is the most-up-to date instruction that we have from Allah. You recite it word for word, and it is not modified. Allah tells you that the Jews and Christians have taken it upon themselves to change the word. They claim that their altered Scriptures are from God, but they make that boast to gain material rewards in this world. Hasn't enough been revealed to you through Mohammed to stop you from asking them anything? I never see any of them asking you about your revelations."

M037,6666 Mohammed: "Allah will use a Christian or Jew to substitute for a Muslim in Hell."

Some rats are changed Jews.

M042,7135 Mohammed: "A tribe of Jews disappeared. I do not know what became of them, but I think they changed and became rats. Have you noticed that a rat won't drink camel's milk, but it will drink goat's milk?"

The next hadith marks the beginning of religious apartheid in Arabia. To this day there are no churches, temples, or synagogues in Arabia.

Bukhari3,39,531 Umar drove the Christians and the Jews from Arabia. Mohammed defeated the Jews at Khaybar and gave ownership of the land to Allah, the Muslims, and Mohammed. But now Umar wished to evict the Jews. The Jews, however, asked to remain on the condition that they provide the labor to sustain the city and in return they would receive half of the proceeds. Mohammed said, "You may stay under those conditions until we change our minds." They remained in Arabia until Umar expelled them from the land [about six years after Mohammed's death].

THE JEWS AS DHIMMIS

What is important about these hadiths is that they established the relationship between Islam and the Jews. The Jews were the first dhimmis, and that was their only relationship with Islam for 1400 years until the establishment of Israel in 1947.

The image one usually has of the Jews in Islam's golden era is that they were respected and honored scholars functioning at a high level in society. The court physician was a Jew, and Jews were among the wise councilors who served the caliph or sultan. There is some truth in this image, but the Jews were never a threat to Islam as they had no real political power. Having no real political power, they were not as persecuted as other Kafirs were.

However, given the dual nature of Islam, this golden picture had vast exceptions. All the rules of a dhimmi fell on the Jew as well as the Christian. In North Africa, the Jews did all the unclean work: they cleaned the cesspools and were tanners, butchers, and hangmen. They even had the task of drying the sewage from the cesspools for sale as fuel. The Jew was inferior; the Muslim was superior.

A Muslim was not to massage a Jew, nor throw away his refuse nor clean his latrines. The Jew are better fitted for such trades, since they are the trades of those who are vile. A Muslim should not attend to the animal of a Jew, nor serve him as a muleteer, nor hold his stirrup. If any Muslim is known to do this, he should be denounced.[1]

Humiliation and contempt were an important part of the ethic in relating to Jews. The favorite epitaph for a Jew was the one Mohammed used, "apes." Dhimmis were never to have higher status than Muslims.

And it was not wise for a Jew to enter into any theological discussions about Islam. Here is a comment about the Jews of Egypt in the 19th century by Edward Lane:

---

1. Ibn Abdun, *Risala fil-qadq wal-hisba*, ed. E. Levi-Provencal (Cairo, 1955), 43ff.

At present, they are less oppressed; but still they scarcely ever dare to utter a word of abuse when reviled or beaten unjustly by the meanest Arab or Turk; for many a Jew has been put to death upon a false and malicious accusation of uttering disrespectful words against the Koran or the Prophet.[1]

This treatment was for all People of the Book, Jews and Christians. This scene is from Turkey in 1908:

The attitude of the Moslems towards the Christians and Jews, to whom, as stated above, they are in a majority of ten to one, is that of a master towards slaves whom he treats with a certain lordly tolerance so long as they keep their place. Any sign of pretension to equality is promptly repressed. It is often noticed in the street that almost any Christian submissively makes way even for a Moslem child. Only a few days ago the writer saw two respectable-looking, middle-aged Jews walking in a garden. A small Moslem boy, who could not have been more than eight years old, passed by and, as he did so, picked up a large stone and threw it at them—and then another—with the utmost nonchalance, just as a small boy elsewhere might aim at a dog or bird. The Jews stopped and avoided the aim, which was a good one, but made no further protest.[2]

Islam could treat the dhimmi Jews in one of two ways, both equally acceptable. They could be physicians in the court of the caliph or they could be "apes" at which a small boy tossed a rock. Both roles are supported by the Koran of Mecca and the Koran of Medina, continuing the dualistic nature of Islam.

THE JEWS OF MEDINA

When Mohammed came to Medina about half the town was Jewish. There were three tribes of Jews and two tribes of Arabs. Almost none of the Jews had Hebrew names. They were Arabs to some degree. At the same time many of the Arabs' religious practices contained elements of Judaism. The Jews were farmers and tradesmen and lived in their own fortified quarters. In general they were better educated and more prosperous than the Arabs.

1. Edward William Lane, *An Account of the Manners and Customs of the Modern Egyptians*, 5th ed. (London, 1871), 305.
2. H.E. Wilkie Young, "Notes on the City of Mosul," enclosed with dispatch no. 4, Mosul, January 28, 1909, in F.O. 195/2308; published in *Middle Eastern Studies* 7 (1971): 232.

Before Mohammed arrived, there had been rivalry and killing among the tribes. The last battle had been fought by the two Arab tribes, but each of the Jewish tribes had joined the battle with their particular Arab allies. In addition to that tension between the two Arab tribes, there was a tension between the Jews and the Arabs. The division of the Jews and fighting on different sides was condemned by Mohammed. The Torah preached that the Jews should be unified, and they failed in this.

All of these quarrelsome tribal relationships were one reason that Mohammed was invited to Medina. But the result was further polarization, not unity. The new split was between Muslims and those Arabs and their Jewish partners who resisted Islam.

Ishaq351 About this time, the leaders of the Jews spoke out against Mohammed. The rabbis began to ask him difficult questions. The doubts and questions were about his doctrine concerning Allah. Doubts about Allah, of course, were evil. However, two of the Jewish Arabs joined with Mohammed as Muslims. They believed him when he said that he was the Jewish prophet that came to fulfill the Torah[1].

THE REAL TORAH IS IN THE KORAN

Mohammed said repeatedly that the Jews and Christians corrupted their sacred texts in order to conceal the fact that he was prophesied in their scriptures. The stories in the Koran are similar to those in the Jewish scriptures, but they make different points. In the Koran, all of the stories found in Jewish scripture indicated that Allah destroyed those cultures that did not listen to his messengers. According to Mohammed, the scriptures of the Jews were changed to hide the fact that Islam was the true religion.

Ishaq364 But the Jews did not believe that Mohammed was a prophet. As a result, they were in error and cursed by Allah. By denying Mohammed's prophethood they conspired against him and Islam.

Ishaq367 According to Mohammed, he was the final prophet. His coming was predicted in the original Torah. Up to this point, Allah had blessed the Jews and protected them, but now they refused to believe the final and ideal prophet. Mohammed claimed the Jews were not ignorant, but deceitful—that the Jews knew the truth about Mohammed, covered the truth and hid it with lies.

Koran2:40 *Children of Israel! Remember the favor I have given you, and keep your covenant with Me. I will keep My covenant with you. Fear My power.*

---

1. The Torah: Genesis, Exodus, Leviticus, Numbers and Deuteronomy.

Believe in what I reveal [the Koran], which confirms your Scriptures, and do not be the first to disbelieve it. Do not part with My revelations for a petty price. Fear Me alone. Do not mix up the truth with lies or knowingly hide the truth [Mohammed said the Jews hid their scriptures that foretold Mohammed would be the final prophet].

Ishaq367 The Koran repeats the many favors that Allah has done for the Jews. They were the chosen people, delivered from slavery under the pharaoh, given the sacred Torah and all they have ever done is to sin. They have been forgiven many times by Allah, and still, they are as hard as rocks and refuse to believe Mohammed. They have perverted the Torah after understanding it.

Ishaq369 The Sira and the Koran claim that the Jews' sins were so great Allah changed them into apes. Still they would not learn and refused to admit that Mohammed is the prophet. They knew full well the truth and hid it and confused others. Even when they said to Mohammed they believed, they concealed their resistance.

Koran2:63 *And remember, Children of Israel, when We made a covenant with you and raised Mount Sinai before you saying, "Hold tightly to what We have revealed to you and keep it in mind so that you may guard against evil." But then you turned away, and if it had not been for Allah's grace and mercy, you surely would have been among the lost. And you know those among you who sinned on the Sabbath. We said to them, "You will be transformed into despised apes." So we used them as a warning to their people and to the following generations, as well as a lesson for the Allah-fearing.*

AN OMINOUS CHANGE

Ishaq381 In Mecca, Mohammed spoke well of the Jews, who were very few. In Medina there were many Jews and his relations with them were tense. Up to now Mohammed had led prayers facing in the direction of Jerusalem. Now the *kiblah*, direction of prayer, was changed to the Kabah in Mecca. Some of the Jews came to him and asked why he had changed the direction of prayer, since he claimed to follow the religion of Abraham.

Since Islam is the successor to Judaism, Allah was the successor to Jehovah. Mohammed preached that it was actually Allah who had been the deity of the Jews but the Jews had deliberately hidden this fact with corrupted scriptures. For this the Jews would be cursed.

Koran2:159 *Those who conceal the clear signs and guidance [Mohammed said that the Jews corrupted the Scriptures that predicted his prophecy] that We have sent down after We have made them clear in the Scriptures for mankind, will receive Allah's curse and the curse of those who damn them.*

Koran62:5 *Those to whom the Torah was given and do not follow it can be compared to a donkey who is made to carry a load of books but is unable to understand them. Those who reject Allah's revelations are a sorry example. Allah does not guide those who do wrong.*

THE AFFAIR OF THE JEWS OF QAYNUQA

Ishaq545 There were three tribes of Jews in Medina. The Beni Qaynuqa were goldsmiths and lived in a stronghold in their quarters. The Sira says that they broke the treaty that had been signed when Mohammed came to Medina. How they did this is not detailed.

Ishaq545 Mohammed assembled the Jews in their market and said: "Oh Jews, be careful that Allah does not bring vengeance upon you like what happened to the Quraysh. Become Muslims. You know that I am the prophet that was sent you. You will find that in your scriptures."

Ishaq545 They replied: "Oh Mohammed, you seem to think that we are your people. Don't fool yourself. You may have killed and beaten a few merchants of the Quraysh, but we are men of war and real men."

Ishaq546 Some time later Mohammed besieged the Beni Qaynuqa in the their quarters. None of the other two Jewish tribes came to their support. Finally the Jews surrendered and expected to be slaughtered after their capture.

Ishaq546 But an Arab ally bound to them by a client relationship approached Mohammed and said, "Oh Mohammed deal kindly with my clients." Mohammed ignored him. The ally repeated the request and again Mohammed ignored him. The ally grabbed Mohammed by the robe and enraged Mohammed who said, "Let me go!" The ally said, "No, you must deal kindly with my clients. They have protected me and now you would kill them all? I fear these changes." Mohammed exiled the Jews and took all of their wealth and goods.

THE CHRISTIANS

THE FINAL STATE OF CHRISTIANS AND JEWS

Islam asserted that Christians had hidden the prophesies that said Mohammed would come to fulfill the work of Christ. To believe in the divinity of Christ is to refuse to submit to Islam. Those Christians who believe in the divinity of Christ and refuse to submit to Islam are Kafirs and infidels. Like the Jews, only those Christians who submit to Islam, become dhimmis and are ruled by the Sharia (Islamic law) are actual Christians. Islam defines all religions and only Islam can talk about Islam.

> Koran5:72 *The Kafirs say, "Jesus is the Messiah, Son of Mary," for the Messiah said, "Oh, Children of Israel, worship Allah, my Lord and your Lord." Whoever will join other gods with Allah, He will forbid him in the Garden, and his abode will be the Fire. The wicked will have no helpers. They surely blaspheme who say, "Allah is the third of three [the Trinity]," for there is no god except one Allah, and if they do not refrain from what they say, a grievous penalty will fall on those who disbelieve. Will they not turn to Allah and ask His forgiveness? For Allah is forgiving and merciful.*

Under Islam, Christians can revere Jesus, but they must accept Mohammed as the final prophet. He is superior to Jesus. The New and Old Testaments must be seen as corrupted and weak. Any conflict between the Koran and the Bible is because the Bible is wrong. The Koran is absolutely perfect and the Bible was changed to cover up its prophecies of Mohammed. Jesus must be no more important than Noah.

This is the Christianity accepted by Islam. This is what Islam calls the "real" Christianity. Islam sees all other forms of Christianity as profoundly wrong.

JIHAD AND CHRISTIANITY

How did 60,000,000 Christians die in jihad? How did 210,000,000 other Kafirs die in jihad?

THE DHIMMITUDE OF THE CHURCH

Mohammed said that silence is consent. The churches in Islamic lands suffer quietly. They have learned that the suffering is lessened if they stay silent. Of course, silence means that they will never escape dhimmitude and over the long haul are doomed.

But the churches in America have been dhimmitized as well. What else explains how the world's largest religion is poor in knowledge and so un-curious?

THE CRUSADES

Here is the media version (same as the university version):

The Crusades are the reason that Muslims don't like Kafirs. The Crusades were lead by demonic, power-crazed popes. They were religious wars led by religious zealots. The Crusades are the worst of the West and the only good was that ignorant Europeans got to meet the enlightened, Golden-Aged Muslim scholars who taught the Kafirs how to be civilized. It was led by evil Christians who left a black stain on all white people. There was no violence in the Middle East until the Crusades.

The truth is a little different than that. Let's start with Islam instead of Christianity. (When you read the popular media and the academic versions, notice that it always about the Christians. This has two causes— cultural self-loathing and ignorance of Islam. You cannot talk without any information.) Mohammed had no success with the religion of Islam and when he turned to jihad he was overwhelmingly successful. After his death, Islam found no reason to alter what worked. The first step of Islamic violence was for the first caliph, Abu Bakr, to kill all of the Muslims who wanted to leave wonderful Islam. After enough Arabs were killed, the survivors found themselves very well satisfied with being alive and being Muslims. (It beat being a dead Kafir.)

When Umar came to power as the second caliph, he did what came naturally. He had been with Mohammed for ten years of jihad and with Abu Bakr for three years of killing apostates, so killing was his nature. Mohammed had tried and failed in his attack on Christian Middle East. Umar took the Christian world by a storm of jihad. Syria, Iraq, Egypt and the rest fell to the sword.

This is worth repeating. The Christians were literally sitting at home and not bothering anybody, when Islam attacked. The Christians were no more to blame than the Jews of Khaybar were when Mohammed left

46

Medina and went 100 miles to attack them. IT ALL STARTED WITH JIHAD.

But the jihad did not stop and soon North Africa, Spain and Asia Minor (what has degenerated into Turkey of today) became Islamic. All Christians and Jews became dhimmis. Dhimmis cannot testify in court, must defer to Muslims socially, cannot display any Christian symbols and pay the jizya tax. A dhimmi could not even defend himself from being struck. Church bells couldn't be rung and if the church needed a roof, the elders had to go to Muslims and grovel and pay extra for the right of repairing the roof. The rape of a Kafir woman by a Muslim was not a legal offence.

This was the state of the Christian world. The emperor of what was left of the Byzantine empire asked for help from the European Catholics. This is what started the Crusades. Four centuries of the rape of women, theft, killing and torture made the Arab Christians cry out for relief. The Crusades were purely defensive in their origins.

About two-thirds of ancient Christianity had disappeared under jihad by the time Europeans decided to go to the aid of the Christians in the Middle East. This leads up to another misconception about the Crusades: that the Christians who participated were bums, robbers and thieves who were looking to enrich themselves. The average Crusader was landed and wealthy. To be a Crusader required a man who could outfit himself with the tools and weapons of war and the supporting comrades. Every soldier requires a lot of help to be on the front line. In an army of today, about 90% of the people are in supporting roles for the actual combat. Rather than making a man rich, being a Crusader made a man poor.

Why did the Crusader do it? According to charters left behind in which Crusaders documented their intentions, they joined the Crusades as an act of penance and for love of fellow Christians in Jerusalem.

THE FIRST CRUSADE

The First Crusades chances of success were slim to none. It was a group of knights without central command, no leader and no real strategy. Yet in 1098 they restored Necaea and Antioch to Christian rule, then in 1099 they captured Jerusalem.

What went wrong? One band of Crusaders went along the Rhine and killed Jews.

THE SECOND CRUSADE

When part of the Christian lands were recaptured, Europe sent out another Crusade. It failed since most of the men died on the way due to starvation and cold weather.

THE THIRD CRUSADE

This Crusade was complicated by divisions of leadership. Richard the Lionhearted was successful in battles, but never recaptured Jerusalem. While he was busy with that, the King of France left the Crusade to go back to Europe and take control of Richard's holdings.

THE FOURTH CRUSADE

The Crusaders became involved with Byzantine politics of which they had no understanding and helped a new ruler to the Byzantine throne. When he would not pay the agreed upon price for the Crusaders' help, they sacked Constantinople. This drove an wedge between the Catholics and the Eastern Orthodox sect which still exists today. It weakened Constantinople and helped to set up the conquest of Constantinople by jihad later.

There were more Crusades, but they all came to nothing. What actually slowed the advance of Islam, in a sense, was the Renaissance. It catapulted Christian Europe ahead of Islam both intellectually and economically.

Today, we curl our lips at religious wars and feel morally superior to those involved in such. Of course, jihad is the exception, which our culture manages to excuse. But a question to ask is, what are we doing about the continued jihad against Kafirs today? In short, the Crusaders tried, what are you doing?

If you would like to learn the real story of the Crusades, not the version that is popular today, read Robert Spencer's *Politically Incorrect Guide to the Crusades*.[1]

---

1. *The Politically Incorrect Guide to the Crusades*, Robert Spencer, Regnery Publishing, 2005.

THE DHIMMIS

DHIMMITUDE

Mohammed took his army a hundred miles from Medina to Khaybar and attacked the Jews. Islam was totally victorious. After taking the property of the Jews as the spoils of war, the Muslims made an agreement called a *dhimma,* with the Jews in Arabia. The Jews could stay and farm the land if they gave Islam half their profits. They then became dhimmis who were under the protection of Islam.

Thus the word dhimmi came to mean permanent, second-class Kafir citizens in a country ruled by Islam. Dhimmis paid a special tax, and their civil and legal rights were greatly limited. The only way out of being a dhimmi was to convert to Islam or flee. The taxes from the dhimmis made Islam rich.

There are very few hadiths about dhimmitude, but it was another of Mohammed's unique political inventions. The scorched-earth policy of killing all nonbelievers had an inherent problem: once everyone was killed, the warrior had to find other work. Mohammed therefore created the policy of dhimmitude to deal with the Jews. Dhimmitude was expanded later to include Christians, Magians, and others.

Dual ethics ares at the very core of the concept of dhimmitude. Political subjugation of Kafirs can only come about by viewing them as separate and apart from Allah's true human beings, Muslims.

It can be argued that the glory of Islam came not from Islam but its dhimmis' wealth and knowledge. The dhimmis were the scholars, since the Arabs of Mohammed's day were barely literate and their classical literature was oral poetry. The secular knowledge of Islam came from the Christians, Persians, and Hindus.

Islam is credited with saving the knowledge of the Greeks from extinction. This is ironic in two ways. First, it was the jihad against the Byzantine/Greek culture that caused its collapse. Secondly, it was the Christian Syrian dhimmis who translated all of the Greek philosophers into Arabic.

The Hindu numbering system was credited to Islam. The Muslims took the numbering system from the Hindus (including the concept of zero) and today we call our numbers Arabic numerals (before that we used the Roman numerals). From carpets to architecture, the Muslims took the ideas of the dhimmis and obtained historical credit. The lists of great Islamic scholars includes the dhimmis with Arabic names living under Islamic dominance.

Over time, as the dhimmi population decreased, the "Golden Age" of Islam disappeared. There has never been a totally Islamic culture that was golden, brilliant or prosperous. To date there have only been eight Nobel prizes given to Muslims in the sciences. All of these were given for work done with Kafirs in Kafir countries. There has never been a scientific Nobel prize given for work in a Muslim country. For that matter, roughly half of all Arabs are still illiterate.

Without the dhimmis, Islam is poor. The total economic output of all Arab countries (without the oil) is equal to that of Spain.

The dhimmis produced the wealth of Islam.
Bukhari4,53,388 Juwairiya said to Umar, "Oh, Caliph, give us your advice." Umar said, "You should continue the arrangement made by Mohammed regarding the dhimmis because the taxes they pay fund your children's future."

Dhimmitude means serving the Muslim masters.
Bukhari3,39,521 Mohammed made an agreement with the Jews of Khaybar that allowed them to use the land in exchange for half of each harvest. Mohammed would give each of his wives one hundred wasqs [a wasq is a camel-load], twenty wasqs of barley and eighty wasqs of dates. Upon becoming caliph, Umar gave Mohammed's wives the choice of continuing the practice, or assuming ownership of the land. Some wanted the land, while others chose the wasqs. Aisha wanted the land.

So the progression was as follows: first jihad, then dhimmitude, and then the destruction of the native dhimmi culture. This became the model for the next 1400 years. The dhimmi became a second-class citizen in Islam and paid a heavy poll tax called the *jizya*. Only Jews and Christians and, sometimes, Magians (Zoroastrians) had the choice of becoming dhimmis. Buddhists, Hindus, and animists (those who believe that the plants and animals of the world are filled with spirits) had the choice of death or conversion.

THE TREATY OF UMAR

The Treaty of Umar (pg. 44) dictated every single aspect of public life for the dhimmi. It is hard to describe the world of the dhimmi. Islam dominated all public space. The government was Islamic; the education was Islamic; dress was Islamic; literature was Islamic. Only inside the dhimmi's house could there be no Islam. The word of a dhimmi could not be used in court against a Muslim and crimes against dhimmis were rarely prosecuted.

The wealth of Islam came from the wealth and labor of the subjugated dhimmis. This had been true ever since Mohammed sent out his first jihadists to raid a Meccan caravan. From that day onward, Islam became wealthy through violence against the Kafir. The perfect example of the Jews of Khaybar as dhimmis was used again and again. First jihad took the spoils of war and slaves; then the dhimmi tax system produced yearly wealth. Islam is a political system with a divine license to take what is wanted from *dar al harb*, the land of war.

These rules created a dhimmi culture throughout sixty percent of what had been Christian and European culture of the first millennium. The conquest took less than a century. Dhimmitude resulted in the total loss of the local culture.

The details of what happened varied from country to country. The Zoroastrian and Buddhist cultures collapsed under jihad and quickly disappeared. The Jews survived as the servants to Islam; some Christian cultures managed to exist for centuries before annihilation (as in Turkey), and the Christians in other areas quickly became Muslims (North Africa).

The actual attitude of Islam toward the dhimmis was more contempt than hatred, and over time the dhimmis disappeared. They either left or converted. It was too hard to be a second-class citizen, and the extra taxes were a burden. As time went on, both Christians and Jews became more Arabic in their outlook; they started to treat women as the Arabs did and their customs became more and more Islamic. Finally it was easier to accept Islam as their religion and stop all the pressure and contempt.

A SCHOLARLY VIEW

As individuals, the dhimmis possessed no rights. Citizenship was limited to Muslims; and because of the superior status of the Muslim, certain juristic restrictions were imposed on the dhimmi. The evidence of a dhimmi was not accepted in a law court; a Muslim could not inherit from a dhimmi nor a dhimmi from a Muslim; a Muslim could marry a dhimmi woman, but a dhimmi could not marry a Muslim woman; at the frontier a dhimmi merchant paid double the rate of duty on merchandise paid by a Muslim, but only half the rate paid by a harbi; and the blood-wit paid for a dhimmi was, except according to the Hanafis, only half or two-thirds that paid for a Muslims. No dhimmi was permitted to change his faith except for Islam...

Various social restrictions were imposed upon the dhimmis such as restrictions of dress... Dhimmis were also forbidden to ride horses... and, according to Abu Hanifa valuable mules. The reason for this prohibition was connected with the fact that dhimmis were forbidden to bear arms: the horse was regarded as a 'fighter for the faith,' and received two shares in the booty if it were of Arab stock whereas its rider received one. Dhimmis were to yield the way to Muslims. They were also forbidden to mark their houses by distinctive signs or to build them higher than those of Muslims. They were not to build new churches, synagogues, or hermitages and not to scandalize Muslims by openly performing their worship or following their distinctive customs such as drinking wine...

The humiliating regulations to which [dhimmis] were subject as regards their dress and conduct in public were not, however, nearly so serious as their moral subjection, the imposition of the poll tax, and their legal disabilities. They were, in general, made to feel that they were beyond the pale. Partly as a result of this, the Christian communities dwindled in number, vitality, and morality... The degradation and demoralization of the [dhimmis] had dire consequences for the Islamic community and reacted unfavorably on Islamic political and social life. So far as the dhimmis formed a considerable element in the administration, the general tone of the administration was lowered as a result of the degrading and demoralizing influences at work on them. In political life also the demarcation between the Muslim freeman and the dhimmi was fatal. The existence of large half-autonomous communities embedded in the very fabric of the Muslim state prevented political unity, while the clashing of ideals and standards of life formed a barrier to social unity[1].

---

1. Ann Lambton, *State and Government in Medieval Islam*, 1981, Oxford, pp. 206-208.

WOMEN

There is a major political division between Islam and the rest of the world. The political duality is between Islam and Kafirs.

The personal duality is between the Muslim and the non-Muslim.

The major duality inside Islam is between male and female. There is one set of rules for men and another set of rules from women. If there were no submission, then there would need to be only one rule: men and women would be treated the same. If they are not to be treated the same, then many more rules are needed.

There is only one area in which men and women are treated equally—male and female will be judged on the basis of their lives on Judgment Day. This section lays out the basis for the doctrine that govern the rules, laws and customs for Muslim women.

Only about 9% of the Koran and about 12% of the Sira refers to females. Most of the doctrine is about men. But there is more than enough in the Trilogy to govern the smallest detail in the life of a woman from birth to death.

The Trilogy as a whole is very negative about women. Here is the data on the Hadith:

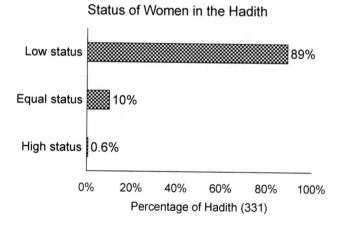

53

WOMAN AS MOTHER

There is only one way in which a woman is held in high status is if, and only if, a woman is a mother, is she held in higher esteem than a man.

> Koran 4:1 *People! Fear your Lord who created you from one soul, and from that soul created its spouse, and from them He spread the earth with innumerable men and women. Fear Allah in whose name you claim your rights to one another and show reverence to the mother who gave birth to you. Allah is always watching you!*

EQUALITY

On Judgment Day both male and female will be judged on the basis of what they have done in their lives. However, as it will become clear from the following material, since a woman must submit to the man in all things, she will be judged by how well she submitted during her life.

> Koran4:124 *As for the believers who do good works, whether man or woman, they will enter Paradise, and they will not be treated unjustly in the least.*

BEATING THE WIFE

Beating the wife is sacred because both Allah and Mohammed sanction it. The Hadith is filled with examples that establish the Sharia law about how to go about beating the wife.

We have part of the code for beating. A woman may be beaten, but not on the face.

> Abu Dawud 11, 2137
> *Narrated Muawiyah al-Qushayri:*
> *Muawiyah asked: Apostle of Allah, what is the right of the wife of one of us over him? He replied: That you should give her food when you eat, clothe her when you clothe yourself, do not strike her on the face, do not revile her.*

This hadith equates camels, slaves and women.

> Abu Dawud 11, 2155
> *Mohammed said: If one of you marries a woman or buys a slave, he should say: "O Allah, I ask You for the good in her, and in the disposition You have given her; I take refuge in You from the evil in her, and in the disposition You have given her." When he buys a camel, he should take hold of the top of its hump and say the same kind of thing.*

Here we have an example of Mohammed striking his favorite wife.

Muslim 004, 2127

...When it was my turn for Allah's Messenger to spend the night with me, he turned his side, put on his mantle and took off his shoes and placed them near his feet, and spread the corner of his shawl on his bed and then lay down till he thought that I had gone to sleep. He took hold of his mantle slowly and put on the shoes slowly, and opened the door and went out and then closed it lightly.

I covered my head, put on my veil and tightened my waist wrapper, and then went out following his steps till he reached Baqi'. He stood there and he stood for a long time. He then lifted his hands three times, and then returned and I also returned. He hastened his steps and I also hastened my steps. He ran and I too ran. He came (to the house) and I also came (to the house). I, however, preceded him and I entered (the house), and as I lay down in the bed, he (the Holy Prophet) entered the (house), and said: Why is it, O Aisha, that you are out of breath? I said: There is nothing.

He said: Tell me or Allah would inform me. I said: Messenger of Allah, may my father and mother be ransom for you, and then I told him the whole story. He said: Was it the darkness of your shadow that I saw in front of me? I said: Yes. He struck me on the chest which caused me pain, and then said: Did you think that Allah and His Apostle would deal unjustly with you?...

THE VEIL

The veil has many manifestations, burka (full body and head covering, complete with a facial "grill"), purdah (isolation of women, including a full body covering), hijab (scarf, but it can include a tent-like robe), but they are all methods of hiding and secluding the woman from society. In no case is there a choice for the woman.

Mohammed's wives were all veiled.

[Bukhari1,8,395] *Narrated Umar: My Lord agreed with me in three things:*

[...]

And as regards the veiling of the women, I said, 'O Allah's Apostle! I wish you ordered your wives to cover themselves from the men because good and bad ones talk to them.' So the verse of the veiling of the women was revealed.

[...]

[Bukhari1,4,148]

The wives of the Prophet used to go to a large open place to an-swer the call of nature at night. Umar used to say to the Prophet "Let your wives be veiled," but Allah's Apostle did not do so. One night Sauda went out at night and she was a tall lady. Umar said, "I have recognized you, O Sauda."

He said he desired that the women might be veiled. So Allah revealed the verses of veiling.

A woman should be hidden from all men. Only their relatives and slaves can know their private lives.

Koran33:55 *There is no blame on the Messenger's wives if they speak un-veiled with their fathers, sons, brothers, nephews on either their brother's or sister's side, their women, or their slave-girls. Women! Fear Allah, for Allah witnesses all things.*

MENSTRUATION

A menstruating woman is unclean and is restricted as to what she can do.

[Bukhari1,4,227]

A woman came to Mohammed and asked, "If anyone of us gets menses in her clothes then what should she do?" He replied, "She should take hold of the soiled place, put it in water and rub it in order to remove the traces of blood and then pour more wa-ter over it. Then she can pray in it."

Menstruation makes a woman unclean.

Koran2:222 *They ask you about women's menstrual cycle. Say: It is a dis-comfort. Therefore, keep away from them during this time and do not come near them until they are clean again. But when they are clean, you may lay with them as Allah has commanded. Allah loves those who turn to Him and seek cleanliness.*

THE STATUS OF WOMEN

It is the nature of females that most of those in Hell will be women.

[Bukhari1,4,184]

[...]

Mohammed's followers then told him that during his prayer they saw him reach out with his hands and grasp something, and later retreat in horror. Mohammed replied, "I saw Paradise and stretched my hands towards a bunch of fruit, and had I taken it, you would have eaten from it as long as this world remains.

I also saw Hellfire, and I have never seen such a terrible sight.
I saw that the majority of the inhabitants were women." When
asked why this was so, Mohammed replied, "They are ungrateful*
to their husbands and to good deeds. Even if you are good to one
of them all of your life, whenever she sees some harshness from
you she will say, 'I have never seen any good from you.'"

Mohammed also saw a woman in Hell being clawed by a cat.
He learned that she had imprisoned a cat, neither feeding it nor
allowing it to seek its own food, until it starved.

Women are less intelligent than men. They are also spiritually inferior
to men.

[Bukhari1,2,28]

Once, after offering prayer at Musalla, Mohammed said to
the women, "O women! Give alms, as I have seen that the major-
ity of the dwellers of Hell were women." They asked, "Why is it
so, O Allah's Apostle?" He replied, "You curse frequently and are
ungrateful to your husbands. I have not seen anyone more defi-
cient in intelligence and religion than you. A cautious sensible
man could be led astray by some of you."

The women asked, "O Allah's Apostle! What is deficient in our
intelligence and religion?" He replied, "Is not the evidence of two
women equal to the witness of one man?" They agreed that this
was so. He said, "This is the deficiency in her intelligence. Isn't it
true that a woman can neither pray nor fast during her menses?"
The women replied that this was so. He said, "This is the defi-
ciency in her religion."

The religion of a woman is controlled by the man.

[Bukhari6,61,572]

Mohammed once said "A woman should not engage in op-
tional fasts without her husband's permission if he is at home."

Women are an affliction to men.

[Bukhari4,52,111]

Mohammed said, "If at all there is a bad omen, it is in the
horse, the woman and the house."

On another occasion, he had said, "I have not left any afflic-
tion after me more harmful to men than women."

Women cannot help their flaws, so be nice to them.

[Bukhari4,55,548]

Mohammed said, "Treat women nicely, for a women is created from a rib, and is much like one. If you try to straighten a rib, it will break, so I urge you to take care of the women."

A woman, a donkey or a dog can nullify prayers.

[Bukhari1,9,486]

When told that a prayer is annulled if the praying ones are passed by a dog, a donkey, or a woman, Aisha said,

Do you make us women equal to dogs and donkeys? While I used to lie in my bed, the Prophet would sometimes come to pray facing the middle of the bed. I felt like it was wrong of me to remain in front of him while he prayed, so I would slip away slowly and quietly from the foot of the bed until I stopped feeling guilty.

Female leadership will lead to political failure.

[Bukhari9,88,219]

During the battle of Al-Jamal, Mohammed heard the news that the people of Persia had made the daughter of Khosrau their ruler. On this, he said, "A nation that makes a woman their ruler will never succeed."

LEGAL

The longest verse in the Koran is about contract law. The general principle in Islamic law is that it takes two women to equal one man.

Koran2:282 ... *Call two men in to witness this, but if two men cannot be found, then call one man and two women whom you see fit to be witnesses. Therefore, if either woman makes an error, the other can correct her. ...*

In this verse about estates, we have another application of the principle that a woman is half of a man.

Koran4:11 *It is in this manner that Allah commands you concerning your children: A male should receive a share equal to that of two females, and if there are more than two females, they should receive two-thirds of what the deceased has left. If there is only one female, she will inherit half.*

JIHAD AND SLAVERY

The use of women for sex after jihad is a constant in the Hadith and the Sira. Here the men are asking about avoiding pregnancy in the slaves. If they were pregnant, they had no value on the market as a slave for sex.

A Muslim is not supposed to have sex with a woman who is carrying another man's child, as per the Koran.

> [Bukhari3,34,432]
> *Once some of Mohammed's soldiers asked if it was acceptable to use* coitus interruptus *to avoid impregnating the female captives they had received as their share of the booty.*
> *Mohammed asked, "Do you really do that?" He repeated the question three times, then said: "It is better for you not to do it, for there is no soul which Allah has ordained to come into existence but will be created."*

Jihad produces slaves and brings in money to finance more jihad.

Ishaq689 When Saed reached Mohammed and the Muslims, the apostle told them to get up to greet their leader. Saed asked, 'Do you swear by Allah that you accept the judgment I pronounce on them?' They said 'Yes,' and he said, 'And is it incumbent on the one who is here?' looking in the direction of Mohammed, and Mohammed answered, 'Yes.' Saed said, 'Then I give judgment that the men should be killed, the property divided, and the women and children taken as captives.'

The Jewish women were later wholesaled as slaves by Mohammed to buy more horses and weapons for jihad.

Remember that the following comes from Islam's sacred texts. Zayd was known as the sword of Allah. Jihad can be ugly:

Ishaq980 When Zayd had raided the Fazara tribe, he and others were injured. Zayd swore he would avenge his injuries. When he was well, Mohammed sent him against the Fazara. He was successful and captured some of the women. One of them was an old woman, Umm Qirfa, whose husband he had killed. Zayd tied a rope to each leg of Umm Qirfa and tied each rope to a camel and pulled her apart. Her daughter was taken captive and passed around to three different men to use as they would for their sex.

MOHAMMED AND SLAVERY

Mohammed was so pure that he would not touch a Muslim woman's hand. This is the reason that many Muslims will not shake a woman's hand. But he would have sex with his slaves. This is an excellent example of ethical dualism. There is not one ethical code for all, but two ethical codes—one for the free Muslim and another for the slave.

[Bukhari9,89,321]

Mohammed used to take the pledge of allegiance from the women by words only after reciting this verse: "...that they will not associate anything in worship with Allah." (60.12) And the hand of Allah's Apostle did not touch any woman's hand except the hand of that woman his right hand possessed. (i.e. his captives or his lady slaves).

MOHAMMED'S FAMILY LIFE

THE LIE

When Mohammed went on his missions to attack those who resisted Islam, he took one of his wives with him[1]. Which one got to go was determined by drawing lots. When Mohammed set out to attack the Mustaliq tribe in Allah's cause, he took Aisha with him.

Ishaq731 [Privacy was a problem when one of Mohammed's wives accompanied him on an expedition. By now the veil had been prescribed for his wives and they were not supposed to be seen or heard. To accomplish this a light cloth-covered howdah was used. Basically this was a box with a seat that could be mounted on a camel's saddle.] On the way back from the battle, Aisha had gone out in the morning to relieve herself. When she got back to the caravan she discovered that she had lost a necklace and retraced her steps to find it. Meanwhile, her tent had been struck and the men in charge loaded the howdah on the camel and off they went, thinking Aisha was aboard.

Ishaq732 When Aisha returned, the entire group had moved on. A young Muslim who had lagged behind the main body of the caravan saw her by the road and offered to put her on the camel he was leading back to Medina.

Ishaq732 When Aisha returned with the young man, tongues began to wag, imaginations worked overtime and gossip spread. Aisha fell ill and was bedridden for three weeks.

Ishaq734-5 Tempers flared and men offered to kill the gossips. Something had to be done. In the end the innocence or guilt of Aisha was determined by revelation in the Koran which to this day is the Sharia (Islamic law) about adultery. There must be four witnesses to prove adultery.

---

1. We do not know the exact number of Mohammed's wives. Some say eleven, others say thirteen. These numbers do not include his sex slaves.

Since there were not four witnesses, then there was no adultery and the gossips got eighty lashes.

Ishaq736 But the scandal did not end here. One of those who got flogged for gossiping was a poet and propagandist for the Muslim cause. The young warrior who had led Aisha's camel was included in a poem written by the poet and it offended him. So he took his sword and cut the poet badly. The poet and his friends managed to bind the young warrior and take him to Mohammed. Mohammed wanted an end to the controversy. He gave the wounded poet a nice home and a Christian sex slave as compensation for the sword blow.

HIS HOUSEHOLD

Islam was no longer poor, indeed, the money from jihad poured in. But Mohammed was a simple man and had little attraction to finery. Hence, his household was poor and the wives complained. The Koran said that they were to obey him. Mohammed did not have to obey the Islamic laws about marriage (a limit of four wives):

Koran33:50 *Messenger! We allow you your wives whose dowries you have paid, and the slave-girls Allah has granted you as spoils of war, and the daughters of your paternal and maternal uncles and aunts who fled with you to Medina, and any believing woman who gives herself to the Messenger, if the Messenger wishes to marry her. This is a privilege for you only, not for any other believer. We know what We have commanded the believers concerning wives and slave-girls. We give you this privilege so you will be free from blame. Allah is forgiving and merciful!*

Koran33:51 *You may turn away any of them that you please, and take to your bed whomever you please, and you will not be blamed for desiring one you had previously set aside for a time. Therefore, it will be easier for you to comfort them and prevent their grief and to be content with what you give each of them. Allah knows what is in your hearts, and Allah is all-knowing and gracious.*

Koran33:52 *It will be unlawful for you to marry more wives after this or to exchange them for other wives, even though you are attracted by their beauty, except slave-girls you own. Allah watches over all things.*

MARY, THE COPTIC SEX SLAVE

M425 Mohammed was given two Coptic (Egyptian Christian) slaves. One he gave to another Muslim but he kept one, Mary, who was fair of skin with curly hair. He did not move her into the harem, but set up an apartment for her in another part of Medina. Mary gave Mohammed something that none of his wives could—a child. It was a male child, Ibrahim, and Mohammed doted on him.

M426 The harem was jealous. This non-Arab slave had given Mohammed his best gift. One of his wives, Hafsa, was away and Mohammed took Mary to Hafsa's apartment in the harem. Hafsa returned and there was a scene. The harem was incensed. A slave in one of their beds was an outrage and a scandal. The wives banded together and it was a house of anger and coldness.

M427 Mohammed withdrew and swore he would not see his wives for a month and went to live with Mary. Umar and Abu Bakr were appalled as Mohammed, their son-in-law, had abandoned their daughters for a slave. But at last Mohammed relented and said that Gabriel had spoken well of Hafsa and he wanted the whole affair to be over.

The Koran:

> Koran66:1 *Why, Oh, Messenger, do you forbid yourself that which Allah has made lawful to you? Do you seek to please your wives? Allah is lenient and merciful. Allah has allowed you release from your oaths, and Allah is your master. He is knowing and wise.*
>
> Koran66:3 *When the Messenger confided a fact to one of his wives, and when she divulged it, Allah informed Mohammed of this, and he told her [Hafsa] part of it and withheld part. When Mohammed told her of it, she said, "Who told you this?" He said, "He who is knowing and wise told me."*
>
> Koran66:4 *"If you both [Hafsa and Aisha] turn in repentance to Allah, your hearts are already inclined to this, but if you conspire against the Messenger, then know that Allah is his protector, and Gabriel, and every just man among the faithful, and the angels are his helpers besides. Perhaps, if he [Mohammed] divorced you all, Allah would give him better wives than you—Muslims, believers, submissive, devout, penitent, obedient, observant of fasting, widows and virgins."*

Ibrahim became a favorite of Mohammed, but when the child was fifteen months old, he fell sick. Mary and her slave sister attended the child during his illness. Mohammed was there at his death and wept mightily. Mohammed was to suffer the Arabic shame of having no living male children to succeed him.

MARRIAGE TO HIS DAUGHTER-IN-LAW

Mohammed had an adopted son, Zeid, and went by his house. Zeid was not there and Mohammed went on in the house. He wound up seeing his daughter-in-law, Zeinab, in a thin dress, and her charms were evident.

Mohammed was smitten and said, "Gracious Lord! Good Heavens! How thou dost turn the hearts of men!"

Well, Zeinab had turned the head of the future king of Arabia and she told her husband what Mohammed said. The stepson went to Mohammed and said that he would divorce Zeinab so he could have her. Mohammed said no, but Zeid went ahead and divorced her anyway. In Arabia a union between a man and his daughter-in-law was incest and forbidden. But while Mohammed was with Aisha, he had a revelation and said, "Who will go and congratulate Zeinab and tell her that Allah has blessed our marriage?" The maid went right off to tell her of the good news. So Mohammed added another wife.

> Koran33:36 *And it is not the place of a believer, either man or woman, to have a choice in his or her affairs when Allah and His Messenger have decided on a matter. Those who disobey Allah and His Messenger are clearly on the wrong path. And remember when you said to your adopted son [Zayd], the one who had received Allah's favor [converted to Islam], "Keep your wife to yourself and fear Allah," and you hid in your heart what Allah was to reveal, and you feared men [what people would say if he married his daughter-in-law], when it would have been right that you should fear Allah. And when Zayd divorced his wife, We gave her to you as your wife, so it would not be a sin for believers to marry the wives of their adopted sons, after they have divorced them. And Allah's will must be carried out.*

Since Zeid was adopted, he was not really a son, so there was no incest.

It was about this time that the veil was imposed by command from Allah. The wives became mothers of the faithful and could not marry after Mohammed died.

SLAVERY

LESSON 9

SLAVERY IS NATURAL

The word slave is a positive one in Islam. Every Muslim is a slave of Allah. Mohammed was involved with every conceivable aspect of slavery. The word Islam means submission and a slave is the ultimate expression of submission.

> Koran2:23 *If you doubt what We have revealed to Our slave [Mohammed], then write a sura comparable to it and call your gods other than Allah to help you if what you say is true.*

Bukhari has 42 references to Mohammed as the Slave of Allah.

> [Bukhari4,55,654]
> *Umar heard the Prophet saying, "Do not exaggerate in praising me as the Christians praised the son of Mary, for I am only a slave. So, call me the Slave of Allah and His Apostle."*

Slavery is as natural as breathing in Islam. The word is never used in a negative way in the Koran, Sira or Hadith. Slavery is in the Sunna of Mohammed and part of the Koran.

Slaves are part of the natural order of society.

> Koran16:71 *Allah has given more of His gifts of material things to some rather than others. In the same manner, those who have more do not give an equal share to their slaves so that they would share equally. Would they then deny the favors of Allah?*

DUALITY AND SUBMISSION

Duality is the only way to sustain slavery, and Islam has sustained slavery for 1400 years. Slavery is part of the sacred order. A believer, a Muslim, may not be enslaved. Only the unbelievers, Kafirs, can be enslaved. The duality of believer/Kafir divides all humanity. The Kafirs are fair game and can be attacked, their protectors killed, their wealth taken and the remaining people enslaved. Slavery is Allah's way. If the slave converts to Islam, then freedom is a possibility.

There is one set of rules for Muslims and another set of rules for the Kafirs. The only unifying rule in Islam is that every single human being

64

must submit to Islam. Before that submission takes place the Muslim and the Kafir have nothing in common.

Slavery is a supreme example of Islam's dualistic ethics and submission. Who submits more than a slave?

To understand this verse, you must remember that a Muslim may not be enslaved. The duality of slavery is clearly stated in the doctrine.

> Koran16:75 *Allah gives you a parable. One man is a slave to another; he has no power. Another man has received many favors from Allah, and he spends from his wealth secretly and openly. Are the two men equal? Praise be to Allah. However, most do not understand.*

> Koran39:29 *Allah sets forth a parable: "There is a slave who belongs to several partners and another slave owned by one man. Are the two in like circumstances?" No, Praise be to Allah. But most of them do not know.*

> Koran30:28 *He gave you a parable that relates to yourselves: Do you equally share your wealth with any slave you own? Would you fear your slave as you would fear a free man? This is how We explain Our signs to those who understand. No, you do not. The wicked, without knowledge, pursue their base desires. But who can guide those whom Allah has allowed to go astray? There will be no one to help them.*

BE GOOD TO YOUR SLAVES

It takes a lot of killing to persuade the survivors of a battle to become slaves. Jihad accomplishes this. Part of Islamic duality is the doctrine of how well captive slaves are to be treated after the violent jihad. Slavery is part of the sacred way of Islamic life.

> Koran4:36 *Worship Allah and do not acknowledge any as His equal. Be good to your parents, your relatives, to orphans, the poor, to neighbors both new and familiar, to fellow travelers, wayfarers, and the slaves you possess.*

The key to good treatment after capture is to convert to Islam. "If one has a brother under his command" is the operative phrase in this next verse.

> Bukhari3,46,721
> *Al-Ma'rur met Abu Dhar, and noticed that he and his slave were wearing similar cloaks. When Al-Ma'rur asked him about that, he replied, "Once I abused a man by calling his mother bad names, so he complained to the Prophet. Mohammed said to me, 'You still show some signs of ignorance. Your slaves are your brothers and Allah has given you authority over them. So, if one has a brother under his command (a Muslim slave), one should*

feed him what he himself eats and clothe him like himself. Do not ask slaves to do things beyond their abilities and if you do so, then help them.'

FREEING MUSLIM SLAVES

Freeing slaves has great merit and is approved in both the Koran and the Hadith. However, only slaves who convert are freed. So here we see the great power of Islamic slavery. Kafirs will become Muslims in order to be freed. If they don't convert then their children probably will.

However, merely converting to Islam after being enslaved does not mean the slave is to be freed. Converting is the first step, but the owner may, or may not, free the converted slave.

In the next verse, Allah gives Islam power over its captives.

> Koran8:70 *Messenger! Tell the captives who are under your control, "If Allah finds good in your hearts [if the prisoners convert to Islam], He will give you something better than that which has been taken away from you, and He will show you forgiveness. Truly, Allah is forgiving and merciful." If, however, they plot to betray you, know that they have already betrayed Allah. He has therefore given you power over them. Allah is all-knowing and wise.*

> Bukhari8,73,226
> *Narrated Osama bin Zaid:*
> *[...] When Allah's Apostle had fought the battle of Badr and Allah killed whomever He killed among the chiefs of the infidels, and Allah's Apostle and his companions had returned with victory and booty, bringing with them some of the chiefs of the infidels as captives.*
> *'Abdullah and the idolators who were with him, said, "Islam has now triumphed, so give Allah's Apostle the pledge of allegiance and embrace Islam." Then they became Muslims and were freed.*

Again, freedom comes only after submitting to Islam:

> Ishaq875 During his session there *some of the slaves besieged in al-Taif came to him and accepted Islam and he freed them.* Abdullah said that when al-Taif surrendered, some of them talked about these lost slaves, but Mohammed refused to do anything saying that they were Allah's free men.

Another incident:

Ishaq878 The apostle asked about Malik and they said that he was in al-Taif. The apostle told them to tell Malik that *if he came to him as a Muslim he would return his enslaved family and property to him and give him a hundred camels.* He came out by night, mounted his horse, rode off to join the apostle, overtaking him in Mecca. Mohammed gave him back his family and property and gave him a hundred camels. He became an excellent Muslim.

LEGAL

The slave has no means of redress, nor any basis for legal action of any sort. The slaves rights are all based upon the good will of its master.

The only way to gain any rights is to convert to Islam. Then some of the brotherhood rights can be claimed.

The reason for the tax exemption on horses was jihad. Mohammed gave cavalrymen three times the amount he gave foot soldiers from the spoils of war (the wealth of the vanquished) to build a better cavalry.

Bukhari2,24,542
Mohammed: "Horses and slaves owned by a Muslim are tax exempt."

Muslims could own shares of a slave, just like any other property.

Bukhari3,44,671
Mohammed said, "Whoever manumits his share of a jointly possessed slave, it is imperative for him to free the slave completely by paying the remainder of the price. If he does not have sufficient money for that, then the price of the slave should be estimated justly, and the slave allowed to work and earn the amount that will free him without overburdening him."

An eye for an eye, a tooth for a tooth is the law of retaliation.

Koran2:178 *Believers! Retaliation is prescribed for you in the matter of murder: the free man for the free man, a slave for a slave, a female for a female. If the brother of the slain gives a measure of forgiveness, then grant him any sensible request, and compensate him with a generous payment [blood money].*

There are two ambiguities in this next verse. Do not use your slave-girls as prostitutes "if they wish to remain pure." And what if they don't want to remain pure? Also, there is a loophole, "Allah is merciful." Be all that as it may, the use of slaves for prostitution was common in Islam.

Koran24:33 *And for those who cannot afford to marry, let them stay pure until Allah fulfills their needs from His bounty. In regard to your slaves who wish to buy their freedom, grant it if you see there is good in them, and give them a part of the wealth that Allah has given you. Do not force your slave-girls into prostitution just to gain the wealth of this world if they wish to remain pure. Yet if they are forced to do so, then truly Allah will be merciful.*

MARRYING SLAVES

A Muslim slave is better in the Islamic hierarchy than a free Kafir.

Koran2:221 *You will not marry pagan women unless they accept the faith. A slave girl who believes is better than an idolatress, although the idolatress may please you more. Do not give your daughters away in marriage to Kafirs until they believe. A slave who is a believer is better than an idolater, though the idolater may please you more. These lure you to the Fire, but Allah calls you to Paradise and forgiveness by His will. He makes His signs clear to mankind so that they may remember.*

Koran24:32 *And marry those among you who are single, or an honorable male or female slave. And if they are poor, then Allah will give them riches from His own bounty. Allah is bountiful and all-knowing.*

MOHAMMED AND THE SLAVE CODE

The examples of Mohammed's life form the basis of slave code.

Bukhari3,46,695
Mohammed ordered his followers to free slaves at the time of solar and lunar eclipses.

Bukhari2,24,542
Mohammed said, "There is no tax on either a horse or a slave belonging to a Muslim"

Bukhari2,25,579
Mohammed made it mandatory for every Muslim slave or free male or female – young or old – to pay a small tax, and he ordered that it be paid before the people went out to offer the 'Id prayer. [...]

A freed slave is not fully free, but still has obligations to the master.

Bukhari4,53,397
Ali delivered a sermon saying, "We have no book to recite except the Book of Allah and this written paper from the Prophet

which contains legal verdicts regarding retaliation for wounds, the ages of the camels paid as tax or blood money, and the fact that Medina is a sanctuary. So, whoever commits heresy in it, or commits a sin or gives shelter to such a heretic in it will incur the Curse of Allah, the angels and all the people, and none of his compulsory or optional good deeds of worship will be accepted. And any freed slave who sides with people other than those masters who freed him, without permission from the latter, will incur the Curse of Allah, the angels and all the people, and his compulsory and optional good deeds of worship will not be accepted." ...

A GOOD SLAVE

A good slave is a Muslim and tries in every way to please his Muslim master.

Bukhari3,46,723

Mohammed said, "Three persons will get a double reward:
A person who has a slave girl, educates her properly, teaches her good manners (without violence), then frees and marries her.
A man who believes in Jesus and then believes in me.
A slave who observes Allah's Rights and Obligations and is sincere to his master."

Bukhari3,46,722

Mohammed said, "If a slave is honest and faithful to his master and worships his Lord (Allah) in a perfect manner, he will get a double reward."

For a slave to flee his Islamic master is a sin against Allah.

M001,0131

Mohammed: "If a slave flees his master, Allah does not hear his prayer."

EUNUCHS

Before Islam, the Arabs had the custom of castrating slaves. After Islam was established, the castration was done by the slave trader outside of Islam. Muslims paid more for a eunuch since he could be used in the harem.

Koran24:31 *And tell the women who are believers that they should lower their eyes and guard their purity, and they should not display their beauty and adornments except that which is normally shown. They should cover their breasts with their veils and only show their adornments to their husband, father-in-law, sons, step-sons, brothers, nephews, or their female servants, eunuch slaves, and children who are innocent and do not notice a woman's nakedness.*

LANGUAGE

Islam has a very detailed language for a complete and sophisticated system of slavery.

abd, a slave, usually a black slave. Abd is also the word for any African or any black person.

abiq, a fugitive slave.

amah, a female slave.

ghulam, a modern term for a slave.

ghurrah, a slave worth 500 dirhams.

ibaq, the freeing of slaves.

ibnu baydailjabin, the son of a mother with a white forehead [a free mother].

ibnu jurratin, the son of a free mother.

istilad, a legal term signifying that a Muslim master has freed a female slave who has born his child.

istibra, the waiting period for determining whether the slave is pregnant or not.

itaq, freeing a slave.

khaadim, a servant/slave.

kinn, a slave who is not mukatab, nor mudabbar, nor umm walad, nor mubaad, but entirely unfree.

kitaba, a slave who buys his freedom.

madhun lahu, a slave who can make business agreements for his master.

mamluk, a slave, usually a white slave.

ma malakat aimanukum, that which your right hand (the sword hand) possesses, a slave taken in jihad. Used in the Koran.

maula, a term used in Islamic law for a slave.

mubaad, a slave with several owners.

mudabbar, a slave who is freed on his master's death.

mukarkas, people having slave mothers among their ancestors.

mukatab, slaves who ransom themselves from their master.

mustabad, slave.

mutaq, a freed slave.

mutiq, the master who frees a slave.

qinn, a slave born from slave parents.

raqabah, the term used for a captured slave.

raqiiq, slave.

surriyah, a Kafir woman slave used for sex. She may be bought, taken as a captive, or descended from a slave.

tadbir, a legal term for freeing a slave after the death of the master.

ubudiyah, slavery.

ummu al walad, a legal term for a slave who has borne the master's child.

umm walad, the enslaved mother married to a slave, who gives birth to his child.

wala when freed slaves die, their estate goes to the one who freed them.

zall, a fugitive child slave.

ETHICS

There is one set of ethics for Islam and another set of ethics for non-Islam. Islamic ethics are profoundly and foundationally dualistic. There is no logical possibility of reform of the dualism.

The treatment of Kafirs varies from their being treated well to being beheaded. Both treatments reflect pure Islam. The fluid nature of the duality gives Islamic ethics great power since it totally confuses the Kafir. Many Kafirs will argue that being treated well is the "real" ethical system of Islam.

On an ethical basis there is no such thing as Islamic pacifism. Islam is a civilization of war and violence. The Sira and Koran show that Islam was a failure until it adopted violence. It then became overwhelmingly powerful.

The Hadith (Traditions of Mohammed) is filled with details of the ethics of Islam.

JIHAD

The political system of jihad is based upon ethical dualism. Jihad is a political method with political goals. The goal of jihad is to make the Kafir submit to Islam. The only reason that Mohammed ever attacked anyone was based upon the fact that they had not submitted to his god, Allah.

Muslims kill other Muslims, but that is never jihad. Jihad is reserved for the Kafir. The subtext of Kafir is that the Kafir has offended Allah by rejecting Him. Hence, all jihad is defensive. Jihad is always caused by the offense of unbelief. Jihad is pure political dualism.

BROTHERHOOD

The brother of a Muslim is another Muslim.

> Bukhari8,73,99 *Mohammed: "Worshipers of Allah, do not allow hatred or jealousy to divide you. Live as brothers. It is sacrilege for one Muslim to desert his brother or to refuse to speak with him for three successive nights."*

> Bukhari3,34,366 *Jarir gave an oath to Mohammed that he would always proclaim that there is no god but Allah and Mohammed is His prophet. He also promised to follow all prayer rituals, pay his taxes, hear and obey Allah's and Mohammed's commands, and never give bad advice to another Muslim.*

TRUTH

When deception advances Islam, the deception is not a sin.

> Bukhari5,59,369 *Mohammed asked, "Who will kill Ka'b, the enemy of Allah and Mohammed?"*
>
> *Bin Maslama rose and responded, "O Mohammed! Would it please you if I killed him?"*
>
> *Mohammed answered, "Yes."*
>
> *Bin Maslama then said, "Give me permission to deceive him with lies so that my plot will succeed."*
>
> *Mohammed replied, "You may speak falsely to him."*

Ali was raised by Mohammed from the age of ten and became the fourth caliph. Ali pronounced the following on lies and deception.

> Bukhari9,84,64 *When I relate to you the words of Mohammed, by Allah, I would rather die than bear false witness to his teachings. However, if I should say something unrelated to the prophet, then it might very well be a lie so that I might deceive my enemy.*

Deceit is part of Islamic war against the Kafirs.

> Bukhari4,52,267 *Mohammed: "The king of Persia will be destroyed, and no one shall assume his throne. Caesar will certainly be destroyed and no Caesar will follow him; his coffers will be spent in Allah's cause." Mohammed cried out, "Jihad is deceit."*

Deceit in war:

> Muslim032,6303 *According to Mohammed, someone who strives to promote harmony amongst the faithful and says or conveys good things is not a liar. Ibn Shihab said that he had heard only three exceptions to the rules governing false statements: lies are permissible in war, to reconcile differences between the faithful, and to reconcile a husband and wife through the manipulation or twisting of words.*

Al Tabarani, in *Al Awsat*, said, "Lies are sins except when they are told for the welfare of a Muslim or [for] saving him from a disaster."[1]

TAQIYYA—LYING TO THE KAFIR.

The name for deception that advances Islam is *taqiyya* (safeguard, concealment, piety). But a Muslim must never lie to another Muslim. A lie should never be told unless there is no other way to accomplish the task.

You can tell a lot from language and Islam has the only word—taqiyya—that means sacred deception. This is a measure of the duality of Islam. All of the world is divided into believer and Kafir, *dar al Islam* (land of submission) and *dar al harb* (land of war). Since the ethical system of Islam is based upon this duality, it comes as no surprise that lying is good.

Mohammed advised deceit and lying many times. It is even advised to lie to other Muslims as long as it makes them feel better.

Let's see how this taqiyya takes place today in America. Who told us that Islam is the religion of peace? Who told us that jihad not the "real" Islam? Islam.

When you go to Islamic Web sites, they openly talk about Islam and jihad. When Muslims talk among themselves, Islam is not the religion of peace, but the religion of dominance. These are all just part of dualistic ethics.

A Christian martyr is one who dies rather than lie about the fact that he is a Christian. But if it endangers a Muslim, he may lie about whether he is even a Muslim. This Koran verse came after a Muslim denied his faith to avoid punishment:

> Koran16:106 *Those who disbelieve in Allah after having believed [became apostates], who open their hearts to disbelief, will feel the wrath of Allah and will have a terrible punishment. But there is no punishment for anyone who is compelled by force to deny Allah in words, but whose heart is faithful.*

Think about this. If a Muslim may deny Islam for his personal convenience, then he may freely deny any part of Islam to help Islam. For instance, a Muslim congressman, soldier or cop may swear that he will uphold the Constitution, but he knows that Islam comes first. So the oath is meaningless, because he has a secret reserve.

---

1. Bat Ye'or, *The Dhimmi* (Cranbury, N.J.: Associated University Presses, 2003), 392.

Koran3:29 *Say: Whether you hide what is in your hearts or make it widely known, Allah knows all. He knows all that is in the heavens and earth. Allah has control over all things.*

There is a special form of lying that resembles taqiyya and that is *kitman*. Kitman means to leave out part of the truth. When you take an oath in court, you not only swear to tell the truth but the whole truth. When a Muslim tells a partial truth, that is kitman.

Here is a famous kitman: Muslims say that the real jihad is the inner struggle, the greater jihad. But in the Hadith, only 3% of the doctrine even mentions this inner struggle. So the Muslim who tells you that the real jihad is inner struggle is leaving out the other 97%. He is practicing kitman.

One more kitman example: After 9/11 an imam was asked about the 72 virgins to be given to a jihadist in Paradise. He said that the 72 virgins were part of a medieval tale and not really Islamic doctrine. What he did not reveal was that the Koran says the jihadists will get virgins in paradise, but does not say how many.

POSITION TOWARD OTHER RELIGIONS

Mohammed's deathbed wishes were to create religious apartheid in Arabia and to use money to influence Kafirs for Islam.

Bukhari4,52,288 *Ibn Abbas said, "Thursday, what a momentous thing happened on Thursday!" He then wept until his tears muddied the earth. Then he said, "On Thursday, Mohammed's condition worsened and he [Mohammed] said, 'Bring me a scribe with his tools so that I may leave you instructions that will keep you from going astray.' Those present disagreed with one another, something one should not do in the presence of a prophet. They said, 'Mohammed is gravely ill.' Mohammed said, 'Leave me alone; my condition now is better than what you wish for me.'*

"On his deathbed Mohammed gave three final orders saying, 'First, drive the Kafirs from Arabia. Second, give gifts and show respect to foreign officials as I have done.' I forgot the third command."

SLAVERY IN THE HADITH

It is forbidden to capture a Muslim and make him a slave. If a slave converts to Islam, then there is a benefit in freeing him. But there is no benefit in freeing a Kafir slave. Islamic slavery is a blessing because sooner or later the slave or the slave's descendants will convert to Islam in order to be free.

However, there are still cultural and legal restrictions. All references to the freed person are always accompanied by the term, "freed slave." Also, the freed slaves possessions go to their former owner when they die.

> Bukhari3,46,693 *Mohammed said, "If a man frees a Muslim slave, Allah will free him from the fires of Hell in the same way that he freed the slave." Bin Marjana said that, after he related that revelation to Ali, the man freed a slave for whom he had been offered one thousand dinars by Abdullah.*

CONCLUSION

There is no hadith that ever refers to humanity as one body. Every hadith that refers to humanity is dualistic—divided into Muslims and Kafirs. Islamic ethics are completely dualistic.

Islamic ethics have no place for integrity. Indeed, integrity is not possible within any dualistic system. Integrity cannot be logically defined within a dualistic system. If deceit is a virtue, then integrity is not a possibility.

No one who adheres to dualistic ethics can have integrity. They cannot tell the Kafir the whole truth, and nothing but the truth, about Islam.

THE KORAN

THE KORAN AND PHILOSOPHY

The Koran lays out a complete philosophic system including politics and ethics. Its metaphysics claim that the only reality is Allah and humanity is to worship Him. Human life has been pre-determined by Allah. The highest form of living is to die for Allah in jihad. Death, Paradise, and Hell are the values of Islam. The proper relationship between Allah and humanity is master/slave (Muslims are the slaves of Allah) and fear (there are over 300 references to the fear of Allah, the Merciful).

The epistemology (what is knowledge and how knowledge is acquired) of the Koran and Islam is revelation. But since Mohammed was the final prophet, the door to further knowledge is closed. The Koran is true because Mohammed said it was so.

LOGIC

The Koran advances a logical system. Truth is determined by revelation. No fact or argument may refute the Koran. Islamic logical persuasion is based upon repetition, assertion and threats. Another part of the persuasion is personal attacks against those who resist Islam. The Koran advances its argument through threats against specific people and groups. If persuasion fails, then force may be used to settle the logical or political argument.

Another aspect of Koranic logic is the use of name calling and personal insults to advance the truth. The Koran, with its poetical language and repeated threats of physical violence, bases its logic on emotions. Although its intellectual truth can be contradictory, the contradictions do not need to be resolved. Understanding apparent contradictions is a key to understanding Islamic logic. In unitary logic, a contradiction shows the theory or argument is false. For instance: if I say that I have just fallen into the swimming pool and yet I am completely dry, that is a contradiction. I was in the water, but I am completely dry. So, something is not true.

But in the Koran, a contradiction does not prove an argument to be false. What appears to be logical contradictions are actually statements

77

of duality that offer two true choices, depending upon the circumstances. This is a dualistic logic.

How do we know that the Koran is true? Because it contains the words of Allah. How do we know that these are the words of Allah? Mohammed said they were Allah's words. How do we know that Mohammed is Allah's messenger? Mohammed reported that Allah said that Mohammed is His messenger. This is circular logic.

Another so-called proof of the Koran's truth is that its very existence is a miracle. How the Koran is a miracle is not clear to the Kafir.

DUALITY

The constant theme of Islam's perfect, eternal, and universal Koran is the division between those who believe Mohammed, and those who don't. This sacred division is dualism; nonbelievers are not fully human and fall under a separate moral code.

ETHICS

The ethical system of the Koran is also dualistic. How a person is treated depends upon his being a believer or a Kafir. There is one set of ethics for the believer and another set of ethics for the Kafir. Deceit, violence and force are acceptable against the Kafirs who resist the logic of the Koran. Believers are to be treated as brothers and sisters. Good is what advances Islam. Evil is whatever resists Islam.

POLITICS

The story of the Koran culminates in the dominance of Political Islam. The Koran teaches that Islam is the perfect political system and is destined to rule the entire world. The governments and constitutions of the world must all submit to Political Islam. If the political systems of the Kafirs do not submit, then force, jihad, may be used. All jihad is defensive, since refusing to submit to Islam is an offense against Allah. All Muslims must support the political action of jihad. This may take several forms—fighting, proselytizing or contributing money.

The basis of the Islamic dualistic legal code, the Sharia, is found in the Koran. The Sharia treats Kafirs, including Jews and Christians, as inferior to believers. This legal inferiority is sacred, eternal and universal.

RELIGION

Some English translations of the Koran use the word God instead of Allah. In an English speaking culture the word God is synonymous with the One-God—Jehovah/Yahweh—of the Jews and Christians. However, the meaning of both Allah and Jehovah/Yahweh is based upon their textual attributes. Allah is defined by the Koran. Jehovah/Yahweh is defined by the Old Testament. On a textual basis Jews, Muslims, and Christians do not worship the same God. As an example, red and blue are both colors, but red is not blue. Likewise, Allah and Jehovah/Yahweh are both a One-God, but they are not the same One-God. Allah is not Jehovah/Yahweh[1]. Hence, Allah is the only acceptable term for the One-God of the Koran. All humanity must face a Judgment Day. The only sure way to Paradise and to by-pass Judgment is jihad.

TRANSLATING THE KORAN

Islam frequently claims that the Koran cannot be translated. Most of the Koran is written in a poetic style that is similar to the ancient classical texts such as the Greek *Odyssey*. The *Odyssey* is an epic story that is written in poetry, which makes it possible to memorize it. The Koran is also written, for the most part, in a poetic form that is easy to memorize.

Take an English proverb: "Birds of a feather, flock together." We have the information that a flock of birds only contains one type of bird, but it is written in poetic form. Can "Birds of a feather, flock together" be translated into Arabic? No. But the meaning of "a flock of birds contains only one type of bird," can be easily translated into Arabic.

The poetry of the Koran does not translate, but the meaning of the Koran can be translated. Read many different translations of the Koran and you will find the meaning is consistent across the translations.

So, can the Koran be translated? No. Can the meaning can be translated into any other language? Yes. If the meaning of a particular part of the Koran cannot be translated, then that implies that the concept is not applicable to that language. Or said another way, that part of the Koran would not be universal. But the Koran is very insistent upon the fact that

---

1. Arab Christians also use the word Allah. The word allah is derived from *ilah*, deity or god, and *al*, meaning the. So Allah means The-God. But the meaning of the name Allah of Arab Christians is taken from the Christian scriptures. The meaning of the name Allah of Islam comes from the Koran. The Allah of Arab Christians is not the Allah of Islam. For Arab Christians Allah is the same as Jehovah.

it is universal. So by definition of universal, it follows that the universal meaning can be translated into all languages.

ABROGATION

You hear it all the time: Islam is a religion of peace. But we all know that Islam is behind most of all terror attacks. The Koran contains a doctrine that supports both good and evil, peace and jihad.

These contradictions were noted by the people of Mohammed's day and the Koran advances a doctrine of how to determine which verse to use. The doctrine is called abrogation [in Arabic: naskh].

> Koran2:106 *Whatever of Our revelations We repeal or cause to be forgotten, We will replace with something superior or comparable.*

[There are as many as 225 verses of the Koran that are altered by later verses. This is called abrogation.]

> Koran16:101 *When We exchange one verse for another, and Allah knows best what He reveals, they say, "You are making this up." Most of them do not understand.*

> Koran13:39 *Allah will destroy and build up what He pleases for He is the source of revelation.*

Verse 2:106 contains the secret of determining which verse to use. The replacement verse is the later verse. But the Koran found in bookstores is not laid out chronologically. Instead, the chapters are arranged by length, not time as in the Old Testament or any historical text. But scholars have long ago divided all the suras (chapters) into Mecca (early) and Medina (later). Generally, since the majority of the changes happened when Mohammed became politically powerful, Medina trumps Mecca.

In reality, it is power, not time that decides which verses are used. When Islam is weak, it uses the "nice" verses and when it is powerful it uses the "cruel" verses.

In truth, no verse is ever really abrogated. Any Muslim can at any time use any verse he wishes. Both verses are true, since they come from Allah. Duality is the actual concept, not abrogation.

Since Islam considers the Old and New Testament to be Allah's revelations, then the entire Bible has been abrogated by the Koran. This is one of the reasons that Muslims can be "Bible-proof". They view the Bible as error-ridden, antiquated and broken-down. It is literally, not worth using. Allah has replaced it with newer and better scriptures.

Anyone who tries to interpret the Koran without knowledge of abrogation and duality is incompetent.

The Koran is very clear about jihad. All the jihad verses abrogate the "good" Meccan verses. The "good" verses are used by those Muslims are too weak to do jihad. When immigrants first arrive in the host country [Islam's terms for Kafir lands], they talk about peace and brotherhood, while making demands about civil rights.

As Islam grows in strength the demands increase in scope. As an example: Kafir laws should not apply to Islamic families, only Islamic law will do. All jihad can be divided into pressure and violence. At some point the political and social pressures move into violence. The first forms of violence are crime and riots. An Islamic riot is a battle in a civil war. These are taking place now in Europe. Europeans, who are as ignorant as American Kafirs, see them as civil rights demonstrations, not jihad.

These are only some of the jihad verses. The Koran uses the term "fighting in Allah's cause" for jihad.

Koran2:244 *Fight for Allah's cause [jihad] and remember that He hears and knows everything.*

Koran2:245 *Who will lend Allah a generous loan, which He will pay back multiple times? Allah gives generously and takes away, and you will return to Him.*

Cut off Their Heads

Koran47:4 *When you encounter the Kafirs on the battlefield, cut off their heads until you have thoroughly defeated them and then take the prisoners and tie them up firmly. Afterward, either allow them to go free or let them pay you their ransom until the war is over. This you are commanded. If it had been Allah's will he would have taken out His vengeance upon them, but He has commanded this so that He may test you by using these others. As for those who are killed for Allah's cause [jihad], He will not let their sacrifice be in vain. He will lead them into Paradise, of which He has told them.*

Koran47:7 *Believers! If you help Allah's cause [jihad], Allah will help you and make you stand firm. But as for those who deny Allah, they will be destroyed. He will make their plans fail because they have rejected His revelations. He will thwart their tactics.*

Do Not Be Weak and Offer the Kafirs Peace

Koran47:33 *Believers! Obey Allah and the messenger, and do not let your effort be in vain. Those who do not believe and who prevent others from following Allah's path and then die as Kafirs will not receive Allah's for-giveness. Therefore, do not be weak and offer the Kafirs peace when you have the upper hand, for Allah is with you and will not begrudge you the reward of your deeds.*

Koran47:34 *Those who do not believe and who prevent others from fol-lowing Allah's path and then die as Kafirs will not receive Allah's for-giveness. Therefore, do not be weak and offer the Kafirs peace when you have the upper hand for Allah is with you and will not begrudge you the reward of your deeds.*

Koran47:36 *Truly this present life is only for play and amusement, but if you believe and fear Him, He will give you your reward and will not ask you to give up your worldly wealth. But if He were to ask you for all of it and strongly urge you, you would become greedy, and this would reveal your hatred.*

Koran47:38 *You are called upon to give to Allah's cause [jihad], but some of you are greedy. Whoever of you acts miserly does so only at the ex-pense of his own soul. Truly, Allah has no use for you, but you have need for Him. If you turn your backs on Him, He will simply replace you with others who will not act like you!*

Stand Together in Battle Array like a Solid Wall

Koran61:1 *All that is in the heavens and earth gives praise to Allah for He is mighty and wise.*

Koran61:2 *Believers! Why do you say you do things that you never actu-ally do? [At the battle of Uhud, some who had pledged courage fled and failed to fight.] It is most hateful in Allah's sight when you say one thing and yet do another.*

Koran61:4 *Truly Allah loves those who fight for His cause and stand to-gether in battle array like a solid wall.*

Fight Valiantly for Allah's Cause

Koran61:10 *Believers! Should I show you a profitable exchange that will keep you from severe torment? Believe in Allah and His messenger and fight valiantly for Allah's cause [jihad] with both your wealth and your lives. It would be better for you, if you only knew it!*

Koran61:12 *He will forgive you of your sins and lead you into Gardens beneath which rivers flow. He will keep you in beautiful mansions in the Gardens of Eden. That is the ultimate triumph. And He will give you other blessings for which you long: help from Allah and a swift victory. Give the good news to the believers.*

Seize Them and Kill Them Wherever They Are

Koran4:91 *You will also find others who seek to gain your confidence as well as that of their own people. Every time they are thrown back into temptation, they fall into it deeply. If they do not keep away from you or offer you peace or withdraw their hostilities, then seize them and kill them wherever they are. We give you complete authority over them.*

When You Travel Abroad to Fight for Allah's Cause

Koran4:94 *Believers! When you travel abroad to fight for Allah's cause [jihad], be discerning, and do not say to everyone who greets you, "You are not a believer," only seeking the fleeting joys of this world [by killing the Kafirs and taking their property]. With Allah are abundant joys. You too were like them before Allah granted His grace to you. Therefore, be perceptive; Allah knows all that you do.*

Koran4:95 *Believers who stay at home in safety, other than those who are disabled, are not equal to those who fight with their wealth and their lives for Allah's cause [jihad]. Allah has ranked those who fight earnestly with their wealth and lives above those who stay at home. Allah has promised good things to all, but those who fight for Him will receive a far greater reward than those who have not. They will be conferred ranks especially from Him, along with forgiveness and mercy, for Allah is forgiving and merciful.*

Do Not Relent in Pursuing the Enemy

Koran4:100 *Those who leave their homes for Allah's cause [jihad] will find many places of refuge and provisions in the earth. Those who leave their homes flying to fight for Allah and His Messenger and die, their reward from Allah is assured. Allah is gracious and merciful!*

Koran4:101 *When you go forth through the land for war, you will not be blamed if you cut your prayers short because you fear that the Kafirs are about to attack you for the Kafirs are your undoubted enemies.*

Koran4:102 *And when you [Mohammed] are with the believers conducting prayer, let a group of them stand up with you, taking their weapons with them. After they have prostrated themselves, let them go back to the rear and allow another group to come up and pray with you, also allowing them to be armed. It would please the Kafirs if you failed to carry your weapons and luggage so that they could attack you all at once. You will not be blamed if you lay down your weapons when a heavy rain impedes you or when you are sick, but you must always be vigilant. Allah has prepared a disgraceful torment for the Kafirs.*

Koran4:103 *And when you have finished your prayers, remember Allah when you are standing, sitting, and lying down. But when you are free from danger, attend to your prayers regularly for prayer at certain times is commanded for believers.*

SUBMISSION AND DUALITY

Political Islam is based upon two principles—submission and duality. Islam divides all of the world into those who believe Mohammed and those who don't. Islam then says that every public aspect [law, education, the media, art ...] of those who do not believe in Mohammed must submit to Islam.

Everything in Islam is based upon dualism. Its fundamental statement is:

1. There is no god but Allah
2. Mohammed is his prophet.

Being a Muslim depends upon belief in two things, Allah and Mohammed, not one. Islam is the practice of duality, but with one god.

KAFIR

The language of Islam is dualistic. As an example, there is never any reference to humanity as a unified whole. Instead there is a division into believer and *Kafir*. Humanity is not seen as one body, but is divided into those who believe Mohammed is the prophet of Allah and those who don't.

DUALITY

Dualism divides all of the universe into halves such as believer-Kafir. But Islam never divides equals. One side must submit to the other. A believer is not equal to a Kafir. The Kafir must submit to the believer.

Dualism divides and accepts contradictions in how to deal with issues. For instance, part of the Koran advocates good treatment of Kafirs. Then a later verse will advocate harm. But this apparent contradiction is resolved by the fact that Allah gave both verses, so they are both true. The later verse is merely the stronger one. Duality allows both sides of a contradiction to be both true.

Submission assures that one side of the duality rules over the other. It is the goal of Islam that all Kafirs submit to Islam. Submission is all about a master/slave relationship.

WHERE ARE THE MODERATE MUSLIMS?

Some terrible Islamic event will occur but the moderate Muslims do not protest the outrage. Then the question is asked, "Why don't the moderate Muslims protest against this behavior?"

The Kafir's favorite theory is that Islam has been "hijacked" by terrorists and that the vast majority of Muslims are "moderates."

Kafirs keep looking to the moderate Muslim to straighten out this Islam "business". Why doesn't this happen? After all, Kafirs will protest when a Kafir does something terrible.

Kafirs want to divide Muslims into "moderate" Muslims and "radical" Muslims. A "moderate" Muslim is one who does not want to harm someone. A "radical" Muslim is a terrorist.

These names are based upon a lack of understanding of the dual nature of Political Islam. The word moderate has one meaning to a Muslim and another to a Kafir. Inside of Islam, a moderate is one who is moderate with the doctrine. A moderate Muslim is one who follows the Sunna (ideal pattern) of Mohammed. Since Mohammed had a dual nature, the doctrine of Mecca and the doctrine of Medina, so Islam and Muslims have a dual nature.

In Mecca, Mohammed preached a doctrine where violence was limited to Hell. In Medina, Mohammed preached a doctrine of war, jihad.

A terrorist is a moderate Medinan Muslim. Moderation means down the middle. It is Mohammed who defines what is moderate. He used terror, and therefore, terrorism is moderation.

> Bukhari1,7,331 *Mohammed said, "I have been given five things which were not given to any one else before me:*
> *1. Allah made me victorious by awe, by His frightening my enemies for a distance of one month's journey. [...]"*

A terrorist who is like Mohammed is a moderate Muslim. Suicide bombers are moderate Muslims, according to Mohammed.

The nice Muslim at work is a moderate Meccan Muslim. But since the doctrine of Mecca is subordinate to the doctrine of Medina, the Meccan Muslim does not speak out against the moderate Medinan Muslim.

So, the answer to the question, why moderate Muslims don't protest is that there is no need to protest. The Meccan Muslim knows that what the Medinan Muslim is doing is pure Islam. Why would they protest Islam?

The Kafirs are the ones who are confused, not the Muslims. A Muslim who would protest against Islamic terror would not really be a Muslim, but an apostate. Being an apostate is a capital crime in Islam. So even if a Muslim felt like criticizing a terrorist, he would be checked by fear.

Now if you would like to see protests from moderate Muslims, then criticize any aspect of Islam. Then you will see protests from moderate Muslims of both stripes who know that Islam or Mohammed may not be criticized or be the butt of humor. There has never been a Mohammed joke in 1400 years. Humor or criticism of Islam are evil and moderates of both Meccan and Medinan Islam will protest, threaten and sue.

Please note the ethical basis of shared community responsibility that is behind the question, "Why don't moderate Muslims protest Islamic violence?" Muslims do not share our ethics. Islamic dual ethics presume that the Kafirs are to suffer at the hands of Islam. So based on dualistic ethics, Muslims have no reason to give a helping hand. Muslims do not help Kafirs.

So moderate Muslims are doing exactly what they are supposed to do. The Meccan Muslims are quietly supporting the Medinan Muslims, while the ignorant Kafirs sit around wondering, "Where are the moderate Muslims?"

LOVE AND HATE AND DUALISM

There is a concept in Islam called *al-Walaa wal-Baraa*. Walaa is basically allegiance or love (for Muslims). Baraa is enmity or hate (of Kafirs). So the concept is to love Muslims and Islam and to hate Kafirs and their civilization. Walaa and baraa are love and hate, Islamic style.

Since Islam is based upon submission and duality, walaa and baraa are the perfect illustration of duality. To love believers and hate Kafirs is pure dualism. But how important is walaa/baraa? A study of the Koran shows that its priorities are:

· Allah is the only god
· Mohammed is Allah's prophet
· walaa/baraa

It is a core principle of Islamic political doctrine. The Koran devotes over half of its words to how foul and evil the Kafirs are. There is not one good or sympathetic word for the Kafirs. If you don't believe Mohammed, then Allah hates you:

Koran40:35 *They who dispute the signs of Allah [Kafirs] without authority having reached them are greatly hated by Allah and the believers.*

If Allah hates, then a Muslim should hate, as well. This hate is not due to moral failings. No, a Kafir is hated for the simple reason that the Kafir does not think that Mohammed is a prophet. [If Mohammed is not a prophet, then the Koran is fiction, and Islam is meaningless.] In the Sira we find that Islam destroys cultured, wise people of high moral standards because they do not believe Mohammed. It is not personal; it is simply Islam.

The greatest Islamic sin is becoming an apostate (one who leaves Islam to become a Kafir). The hatred of an apostate is another example of baraa.

But Ahmed, the professional engineer in your office, does not say he hates Kafirs. In fact, he says that he loves America. However, if Ahmed is a devout Muslim, then he follows the Koran and it says (in 13 different verses):

> Koran3:117 *Believers! Do not become friends with anyone except your own people.*

How clear can this be? A Muslim should be friends only with Muslims and not with Kafirs—walaa/baraa. If Ahmed is actually your friend, then he is not a Muslim in that moment. If he is a Muslim, then he may be friendly, but he is not your friend. That is the nature of baraa. His contempt is covered with deceit. Mohammed repeatedly told Muslims to use deceit with Kafirs.

Walaa/baraa is the perfect summation of Islam's dualistic ethical system. A Muslim does not kill, lie, or steal from another Muslim. Kafirs are not included in this list. A Kafir may be treated well or a Kafir may be abused, deceived or killed. In Islam, there is no Golden Rule.

Walaa/baraa destroys all empathy and sympathy for Kafirs. The walaa/baraa principle is duality at the personal level while dar al Islam/dar al harb (land of submission/land of war) is duality at the political level. Islam is incapable of being our friend and only loves itself. But how many Kafirs think that if we are good enough to Muslims, then Muslims will love us?

SUBMISSION

Dhimmis were forbidden to study the Koran, and as Kafirs, we have made ignorance of the doctrine our official policy. Consider our submission by ignorance:

- Jews and Christians do not know about the Arabian Annihilation (the elimination of all Jews and Christians from Arabia).

- People don't know that white women were the slaves of choice among Arab, Berber and Turkish Muslims for 1,400 years.
- Blacks in America do not recognize and teach the Islamic origins of their slavery[1].
- Christians don't realize that they lost half their territory and 60 million people to Islam in Turkey, Syria, and North Africa.
- Political Islam destroyed half of Hindu culture.
- Political Islam annihilated most of Central Asian Buddhist culture.
- Islam destroyed all of the native religious culture of Africa in Islamic areas.
- The theory and history of jihad are not taught in any military academy, foreign service school, or law enforcement school.
- No Christian or Jewish school of religion teaches about the political doctrine and history of Islam.
- No school teaches about the Islamic annihilation of the 270,000,000 victims of jihad over the last 1400 years.

What is significant about the Kafir response to Islam is that we are willfully ignorant.

---

1. The African slave traders were Muslims. Their ancestors had been plying the trade of war, capture, enslavement, and sale for a thousand years. Mohammed was a slave trader. Long after the white slave traders quit, the African Muslims continued their slave trade. It still exists today.

THE TEARS OF JIHAD

The story of the destruction of Smyrna found in Level 1 is a routine story in the history of Islam. It is an example of what has been standard practice for 1400 years.

Smyrna was the experience of the 60,000,000 Christians in Syria, Egypt, Iraq, North Africa, Spain and everywhere jihad touched. But it was not just the Christians, it was the Hindus, the Buddhists and every Kafir. Smyrna is the way jihad works. The accounts of jihad in Bangladesh today read just like Smyrna. It is the nature of Islam.

Now you know why Islam does what it does. The "why" is the doctrine of Political Islam. Muslims always try to do what Mohammed did and he succeeded best when he pressed the Kafirs the most. Jihad is Sunna.

But why don't we know how 270,000,000 Kafirs died under jihad? What is the exact history of these deaths?

There is a detailed history, but that history is not taught in any college course. Accepted history talks about the spread of "glorious" Islam. In standard history, Islam invades and the area magically becomes Islamic. No mention is made of death and dhimmitude. No Kafirs were killed in the manufacture of academic Islam.

What is common to Christianity, Judaism, Buddhism, Hinduism and even atheists, that makes us deny Islamic history and doctrine? There is an answer. These cultures all have several things in common with regards to jihad.

- Massive losses of territory and culture
- Millions of deaths over 1400 years.
- The cancer of dhimmitude which grinds down the culture after invasion by war or immigration.
- Islam never regrets jihad, annihilation and terror against these cultures.
- An ethical system based upon the Golden Rule.

Islam has no shame or guilt about its history of terror. This means that Islam is incapable of being corrected. Look at human history. It does not move in a straight line. Humans may have a moral code of high standards, but do we follow it at all times? No, both as individuals and society we make grave errors. When the situation gets bad enough, we can be called back to right behavior by an appeal to our ethics (and force, if needed). Our sense of right and wrong is used to judge us. The Golden Rule is used to bring us back to the right path.

Shame and guilt can be used for correction. Empathy with the victims can be used to make us see our wrongs.

But Islam has not done anything wrong when jihad is used to terrorize and dhimmitize Kafirs. Islam has no empathy, shame or guilt. Muslims never write histories of regret similar to ours which show regret for the Trail of Tears or slavery or racism. There is no such literature in Islam.

THE FIRST WAVE

After Mohammed died in 632, Abu Bakr became caliph. Many of the Muslims wanted to leave Islam, but the Apostasy Wars persuaded them that converting to Islam was a better choice than dying.

In AD 633, Islam began to invade Babylonia (Iraq) and Syria. This lasted about ten years and consisted mostly of small raids in villages. This invasion was helped by the fact that many Arabs already lived in these areas and were easily converted to Islam due to both kinship and the license it provided to plunder and to rape women.

Both the Byzantine and Persian empires were failing and could not deal with the constant raids.

The whole region of Gaza was sacked and devastated in 634. Four thousand Jews and Christians were killed. In 636 we find the first Christian bishops facing destruction by what they called Saracens (Arab Muslims). From the very beginning, Kafirs had no understanding of Islam.

In general, those in towns survived better than those in the villages and countryside.

In Babylonia, monasteries were destroyed, monks were killed and Christians were killed or raped, enslaved and forcibly converted. The operations were carried out by both Muslim Arabs and Kafir Arabs. By 642 Babylonia was in the power of Islam.

In 639, Islam invaded Christian Egypt. Luckily for Islam, the Christians already had a war going amongst themselves. Whole towns were annihilated. The Christians were terrified and fled.

The civil war led some Christians to join the Muslims in order to hurt the "enemy" Christians.

Damascus fell. Khalid, the Sword of Allah, murdered all Christians who could be found in Aleppo and Antioch. Those who survived were taken as slaves.

Palestine was crushed and then jihad entered into Armenia. Armenia was suffering a civil war, like Egypt, where one set of Christians were fighting against another set of Christians. In 642 Islam destroyed the town of Dvin and carried off 35,000 Christian slaves. The next year they returned and destroyed more of Armenia.`

In North Africa, Muslims took slaves and wealth, while destroying the countryside. Tripoli was destroyed in 643, Carthage was razed to the ground and most of the Christians were killed. (Remember, St. Augustine was from Algeria.)

Back in Asia Minor, Anatolia, jihad destroyed churches in Nicaea, Antioch and other cities. The first attempt to destroy Christian Constantinople started in 717.

In 712, Islam invaded Spain from what had become Islamic North Africa. The first shipment of Kafir sex slaves to Africa consisted of 3000 women for sex slaves[1]. Massive immigration of Muslims took the land for their fiefdoms. Kafirs were taken as slaves to work the land.

Jihad invaded across the borders of southern France in 722. Towns were destroyed. The Spanish city of Castile was invaded and put to fire and sword. The remainder of the Kafirs were sold into slavery.

The islands of the Mediterranean and the shipping felt the power of jihad on the seas. The Kafirs of Rhodes and Crete were killed, robbed and enslaved. Naval jihad even went as far north into Europe as Scandinavia. Islamic jihad ravaged all the islands of the Mediterranean.

Islamic piracy was the cause of the first military action by the USA under Jefferson in 1801. That expedition led to the line in the Marine hymn: "From the halls of Montezuma to the shores of Tripoli." So America's first struggle against jihad started in 1801.

THE SECOND WAVE

The Turks invaded the new Islamic empire from Asia. They slaughtered many of the Muslims and took Baghdad. [The Turks were not Muslims at the time of the invasion.] The Turks were a fierce nomadic tribe, even more fierce than the Arabs. The new conquerors became Islamicized and started the destruction of Anatolia.

---

1. *Jihad*, Paul Fregosi, Prometheus Books, 1999, pg 99.

By 1021 Armenia had been devastated and the first of the Byzantine Kafir defeats had occurred. Anatolian Greeks became ongoing prey for the Turks.

In the early 1300's the Muslim Turks were in a constant state of war with Christians in Anatolia. Christians were still busy fighting among themselves. The Catholic Christians hated the Orthodox Greek Christians and so the Greeks were fighting on two fronts. It was a repeat of the Jews' experience in Medina, because they could not stand together against Islam, so the Muslims took them down one a time. The division among Christians has always been Islam's great advantage.

By the early 1400's, Islam had started its invasion of Europe. Then, in 1453, Constantinople was attacked. The murder, theft, and destruction of religious art and the rape of women lasted for days.

The invasion of Europe continued up to the gates of Vienna. Then, on September 11, 1683, the Europeans finally united to drive the Turks back to what had become Turkey.

The jihad into the East is omitted here. The short story was that the Buddhists, Zoroastrians, and Hindus were victims of the same process and with the same result. The Zoroastrians of Persia were annihilated totally.

ISLAMIZATION

It was not the military invasion that destroyed Kafirs. History is filled with invasions that destroyed cities and killed people, but life returned to some normalcy after a generation or two. Islam annihilates the native culture so that it remains Islamic for the rest of time. The military jihad prepared the way for the legal/political jihad.

When Islam first entered the Middle East it was moving fast and had little interest in governing, other than to appoint a military governor. Local customs, procedures and laws remained the same. The middle level officials remained the same. Some locals were actually happy at the conquest. For an example, the Syrian Christians were ruled by the Byzantine Greek Christians and had a different approach to Christianity. The real friction was over theology, not taxes and governance. The Syrians were happy when Islam defeated the Greek Christians. The Syrians saw the conquest as punishment for the way Greeks worshipped. The Muslims did not increase taxes and that was all the Syrians cared about. This contentment would not last, but by then it would be too late to do anything about it. Syrian Christianity was annihilated in the end.

Under the Islamic political system, the tax money was sent to Medina through religious leaders. Political power moved to the local bishops and rabbis. They had to collect the taxes and so the political system became religious and the religious leaders were politicized. At this stage the culture was Christian, but the real power came from Arabia.

So there was collaboration between the minority Muslims and the majority Christians. Everyone still used their native languages. Political power was administrated by native administrators.

These were problems that would lead to Islam's weakening over time, so the Islamic weapon of immigration was used. Muslims began to migrate to the cities of political power.

They confiscated land and added a new tax. These were little jihads with the usual destruction, killing, theft and rape of women.

There was a new problem with the invading Muslims. They all came with their old tribal allegiances and fought among themselves as they had done back home. The locals were frequently experienced collateral damage.

Muslims began to take over the administration and Arabic became the language of government. For instance, a Copt could have his tongue removed if he spoke Coptic to a Muslim administrator. Arabic became the language of power and native languages began to disappear.

Christians and Jews became dhimmis, so they could not be enslaved or massacred. The Treaty of Umar [pg. 61] became the basis of political life. Churches could not be built or repaired without permission. Traveling Muslims could stay at a Kafir's house for free. Dhimmis could not help anyone who opposed Islam and could not read the Koran. They could not discuss religion with a Muslim nor try to convert anyone. They had to wear special clothing and could not carry weapons. Bibles had to be keep out of sight. If any dhimmi hit a Muslim, all dhimmis could be punished.

How a dhimmi was treated depended upon the nature of his Muslim acquaintances. A dhimmi had practically no civil rights. The only function of the dhimmi was to produce wealth for Islam.

The dhimmis were hurt by the constant competition of the flood of slaves from jihad. The dhimmi was always at the short end of the stick. A dhimmi had every reason to end the suffering and become a Muslim. Since Islam controlled all of the public space, the dhimmi adopted the Islamic attitudes about women, justice and a thousand other cultural things. It was an easy step to submit to Islam and live an easier life.

Of course, there were some Christians who submitted to Islam as soon as possible, to even the score with enemies who remained Christian. All of this was played out against a terrible Christian schism over different doctrines. There were wars and intrigues between Christians. Some welcomed Islam as solution to Christian strife.

Put another way, it was politically impossible for Christians to unite against jihad, so all sides were annihilated over time, with each feeling righteous.

In addition to the grinding quality of life as a dhimmi, there were surges of violence where an entire town would be massacred. This violated the dhimmi status, but any excuse could justify it. A common reason for violence was that a Kafir insulted Mohammed.

This was the end of Christianity in the dhimmi areas. It may have taken centuries, but over time Christianity just wore away and left no trace.

In the late 19th century, rising European power forced Islamic countries to drop the formal legal dhimmi status, but it remains in force in a thousand small insults and injuries. The pressure of threats remains today against Christians in Muslim countries.

THE RESULT

The worst part of the enormous suffering and degradation of jihad and dhimmitude is that we have blocked it out of our minds and hearts. We must learn and remember our ancestors suffering or we and our children will repeat it.

Islam annihilates all other cultures. It has done so for 1400 years. Kafirs must come to terms with their history with Islam.

It was not the strength of Islam that caused the Kafir culture to vanish. Islam's greatest strength is its ability to divide and confuse the Kafirs. War usually consists of two elements: killing and propaganda. Islam has no equal in its war of propaganda.

IN ACKNOWLEDGMENT

This micro-history of the early Christianity's destruction is adapted from *The Decline of Eastern Christianity under Islam* by Bat Ye'or.

The story of the destruction of Buddhist, Hindu and other Kafir cultures was the same as for Christianity—annihilation. Buddhism was destroyed along the Silk Road and in what is now Afghanistan. Modern India is about half of the original Hindustan. Jihad has destroyed more human culture than any other historical force.

ARGUMENT

INTRODUCTION

One of the goals of this lesson series is to teach how to prevail in discussions and arguments about Islam. The doctrine of Political Islam provides the strongest argument against Islam. The second strongest argument is the history of jihad.

In debating about Islam do not engage the others' arguments on their points. Instead create a new basis by bringing in facts about Islam's political nature, Kafirs, duality and submission.

Instead of resisting your opponents, use the principle of duality to show both sides of the contradiction. Point out that Islam always has two ways to treat the Kafirs and what you want to do is provide the rest of the doctrine that is left out of the argument—the Kafir viewpoint.

FOUNDATIONAL

Your continual strategy is to stay with Koran and Mohammed. When the other person bring up Christianity, stay with Political Islam If they want to talk about Christianity, say you will compare Jesus with Mohammed, but stay with Mohammed. If they want to talk about the Crusades, say they were in response to the jihad that conquered Christian lands. And jihad comes from the Islamic political doctrine. If you will stay with the foundational doctrine, you will always prevail and persuade.

Nearly every argument you hear is from the media and the media never talks about Political Islam's doctrine. So when you speak about doctrine, you are presenting new material. Your debate opponents have opinions; you have facts. Ask them where they got their arguments. You will be glad to tell them where you get your facts.

When they tell you about what their Muslim friend says, tell them that you have a Muslim friend called Mohammed. Your Muslim friend outranks their Muslim friend. If they get their information from some Muslim expert, the strategy does not change—go to the Sunna of

Mohammed. He is the supreme expert; their expert is second rank, no matter who he is.

It is also a good time to ask if they have any Muslim apostate friends. This brings up the chance to introduce what apostasy means in the Sharia.

When they say that what Muslims do is in response to our failures, colonialism, foreign policy, whatever, show them how everything Muslims do is based upon political doctrine.

All of these case studies are based upon the doctrine of Islam.

CAN YOU READ ARABIC?

Everyone from Muslims to atheists ask if you can read Arabic. The implication is that Arabic is a unique language that can't be translated and therefore, how could you know what you are talking about? First, the Koran claims to be a universal message for all humanity for all times. If the message is universal, then it must be able to be understood by all. If everybody cannot understand the message, then by definition it is not universal. So, which is it?

Another thing to consider is that over half of the Koran is about Kafirs and politics. Do you really think that a political message about a Kafir cannot be understood by the Kafir? If so, what is that message that cannot be understood?

Also, it must be made clear which Arabic is being spoken about. The Arabic of the Koran is classical Arabic which is about as similar to modern Arabic as the English of Chaucer is similar to modern English. Said in another way, not even a modern Arab can read classical Arabic. It is estimated that fewer than a thousand scholars who read classical Arabic can compose a paragraph in classical Arabic script on a random topic.

And what about the billion-plus Muslims who don't understand modern Arabic? If it is necessary to understand classical Arabic to understand what the Koran is about, then how can all those non-Arabic-speaking Muslims understand the Koran? And if they cannot understand the Koran, how can they be Muslims?

Ask the person who presents the argument if they have any opinions about the doctrine of Christianity. Then ask them if they read Hebrew, Aramaic or Biblical Greek? If they do not read those languages how can they form an opinion about something they have to read in translation? Of course they can read it and form an opinion, the same way we can read and understand the Koran.

A secondary question is why would anyone want to believe that the Koran couldn't be understood? What is the purpose of believing that out of all the books in the world, it is the one that cannot be translated and understood?

The Koran is only 14% of the total doctrine[1]. Would the questioner believe that the other 86% of the doctrine not be understood as well?

WELL, THE CHRISTIANS/JEWS DID...

There are two different ways to deal with comments about Christianity and Judaism.

Method A

Reject all conversation that is not about Islam. Reject all comparative religious talk. Insist on talking solely about Islam. If they want to talk about Christianity/Judaism fine, but don't respond, except to say that you want to talk about Islam, not comparative religion. When it is you turn, return to Islam. Refuse to engage in comparisons. Islam must be taken on its own. There is no comparison. Insist on discussing Mohammed and the Koran.

Method B

Ask if they have a reason that they don't want to talk about Islam, since they want to change the subject. The average person knows next to nothing about this subject and sometimes this gambit is merely a way to steer the conversation into a familiar ground.

They are just trying to prove that Islam is not any worse than Christianity. At this point, welcome the chance to compare the two, but choose the ground of comparison. The best place to start is with the founders. Compare Mohammed to Christ. The other good comparison is in ethics. Compare Islam's dualistic ethics to Christian unitary, Golden Rule ethics.

Another version of this argument is that the person will compare some failed Christian to a "good" Muslim they know at work. It is fairly useless to do personal comparisons. How do you choose which Muslim out of 1.5 billion Muslims and which Christian does you choose out of a couple billion Christians?

A variation on the "Well, the Christians did ..." is "What about the Crusades"? This is the time to say you welcome a comparison of the Cru-

---

1   http://cspipublishing.com/statistical/TrilogyStats/The_Relative_Sizes_of_the_Trilogy_Texts.html

sades to jihad. Start with the question of why the Crusades were needed. Islamic jihad invaded the Christian Middle East and subjugated them. The Crusades were a response to a cry for help by the tortured and oppressed Christians in their native land. Did the Christians do some wrong things? Yes, but notice that the Crusades have been over nearly a thousand years. Jihad is active today. And while we are at it, why do academic libraries have many books on the Crusades, which lasted only 200 years, and so few on jihad, which has been going on 1400 years? The West has analyzed the Crusades, *ad nauseam*, and has barely looked at jihad.

I KNOW THIS MUSLIM AND HE SAYS...

Why is the Muslim an expert on Islam? Remember, the average Muslim knows very little about the doctrine of Islam. Why? Because, historically the imams have acted as the high priests of Islam and they have never made the doctrine simple to understand. That is one way they keep their prestige and power.

It does not make any difference who the Muslim is. Once you know something about the doctrine of the Trilogy, you can say that you also know a Muslim, and his name is Mohammed, and what you say comes from the Sunna. In short, your Muslim, Mohammed, can trump your friend's Muslim on any issue of doctrine. If the Muslim your friend knows says something about Islam that agrees with Mohammed, then it is right. If what he says contradicts Mohammed, then he is wrong. Mohammed is the only Muslim who counts.

I KNOW THIS MUSLIM AND HE IS A NICE MAN

So a man is nice and he is a Muslim. What does that prove about Islam? He may follow the Golden Rule and not Islamic doctrine. That is, he may be a poor practitioner of Islam and a good person.

The first question to ask about "nice" Muslims is do they believe in the Koran and the Sunna of Mohammed? They will say yes. Now is the time to explain about the Islam of Mecca and the Islam of Medina. It is also time to explain about dualism and how Islam always has two faces.

Stay with the doctrine and the history of Islam, never get personal and talk about an individual Muslim. Actually, there is one way to talk about any Muslim, just show how what they do and say follows or does not follow the doctrine.

MUSLIMS REJECTING SHARIA

You will discover that some Muslims say that they reject Sharia. What they mean is that they reject some parts of the Sharia. Since Sharia covers the details of the Five Pillars, including prayer, to reject all of the Sharia is to become an apostate.

The first question to ask any Muslim who rejects part of Sharia, is exactly what part they reject. Since the rules of Sharia are based upon the Sunna of Mohammed and the Koran, that means rejecting the Koran and the Sunna. But a Muslim must accept all of the Koran as the exact perfect manifestation of Allah. Therefore, the Sharia that is based on Koran must be accepted as valid. In the same way, Mohammed is the perfect Muslim and is to be imitated in all matters. To reject Sharia based upon Sunna is to be an apostate.

Here is a summary of the proper Islamic attitude about Sharia:

The word Sharia means "road," and the implied imagery of the term is that our life is like a road in a desert, with God the oasis we seek. Thus the primary focus of Sharia law is on humankind's journey toward intimacy with our Creator, and the Sharia's purpose is to establish the links or guideposts between God and humanity. The Sharia is the body of divine guidance, its structure, format, and construct. It is important to Muslims because it is the guide by which the Muslim determines what is good or ethical. To Muslim ears, "Sharia law" means all that is constitutional, ethical, right, and compassionate—the conditions necessary for what Americans call the pursuit of happiness. This is why many Muslims seek to base their national legal systems on Sharia law, for that is the highest authority they can claim on their behalf in correcting wrongs[2].

THAT IS NOT THE REAL ISLAM

When you bring up an atrocity by Islam—the 9/11 attacks, Beslen, Russia, Mumbai India—a common apologist response is that this is not the real Islam. Ask them how they know what is and is not "real" Islam. Real Islam comes from Mohammed and he frequently launched sneak attacks against Kafirs. For example, he attacked the Jews of Khaybar in a surprise raid in the morning (his favorite sneak attack time of day). After he had killed enough Jews so that the rest submitted, he then tortured some to find more buried treasure and his men raped many of the women. That is how Mohammed did atrocities, so murderous sneak attacks against civilian Kafirs is Sunna.

---

2   *What is Right with Islam*, Imam Feisal Rauf, Harper San Francisco, 2004, page 150.

If there is anyway that the event is similar to the Sunna, then it is the real Islam.

If you are quoting the Sharia, then it is the real Islam, by definition, as are the Koran and the Sunna. All other Islam, such as is found in the media, are incorrect.

THEY DON'T REALLY BELIEVE THAT

You reveal some horrific part of the doctrine and the other person says that Muslims don't really believe that. What do Muslims call themselves? The Believers. What do they believe? The Koran and the Sunna. They say that is what they believe. Now ask two questions: have you read and understood the Koran or the Sunna? If not, how do you know anything about what Muslims believe?

I KNOW THIS MUSLIM AND HE IS NOT VIOLENT

This is a restating of, "I know this Muslim and he is good man." He may be a non-practicing Muslim and a good man who follows the Golden Rule.

A non-violent Muslim believes in the Koran and the Sunna of Mohammed. The Koran suggests both violence and tolerance against the Kafirs. Today in America, the power of Islam is just getting started, so Islam is still weak. When Mohammed was weak in Mecca, he did not kill anybody. Islam is still in the first phase of jihad here.

We know from the Sira, that many Muslims just don't have the stomach for the violence. The Sira shows that Muslims can support jihad many ways, besides personal violence. The "peaceful" Muslim you know is commanded to give money to Islamic charities and the charities give the money to the actual fighters.

WHAT ABOUT THE VIOLENCE IN THE OLD TESTAMENT?

Apologists love to bring up the violence in the Old Testament to show that Islam is no better or worse than Christianity and Judaism. This is another version of "I don't know anything about Islam so I will talk about what I do know—Christianity and Judaism.

There is only one way to prove or disprove the comparison; measure the differences in violence.

The first item is the definition of violence. The only violence that matters to someone outside of either Islam or Judaism is what they do to the "other", or political violence. Cain killing Able is not political violence.

Political violence is not killing a lamb for a meal or making an animal sacrifice. Note, however, both are violence for a vegan or a PETA member, but it is not violence against them.

We now need to compare the doctrines both quantitatively and qualitatively. The political violence of the Koran is called "fighting in Allah's cause", or jihad.

We must do more than measure the jihad in the Koran. Islam has three sacred texts: Koran, Sira and Hadith, the Islamic Trilogy. The Sira is Mohammed's biography. The Hadith are his traditions—what he did and said. Sira and Hadith form the Sunna, which form the Sharia, the perfect law of all Islamic behavior.

It turns out that jihad occurs in large proportion in all three texts. Here is a chart about the results:

Amount of Text Devoted to Jihad

Category	Percentage
Complete Trilogy	31%
Hadith	21%
Sira	67%
Koran	9%

Basically, when Mohammed was a preacher of religion, Islam grew at the rate of 10 new Muslims per year. But when he turned to jihad, Islam grew at an average rate of 10,000 per year. All of the details of how to wage jihad are recorded in great detail. The Koran gives the great vision of jihad—world conquest by the political process. The Sira is a strategic manual and the Hadith is a tactical manual of jihad.

Now let's go to the Hebrew Bible. When all of the political violence is counted, we find that 5.6% of the text is devoted to political violence as opposed to the 31% of the Trilogy.

When we count the magnitude of words devoted to political violence, we have 327,547 words in the Trilogy and 34,039 words in the Hebrew Bible. The Trilogy has 9.6 times as much wordage devoted to political violence as the Hebrew Bible.

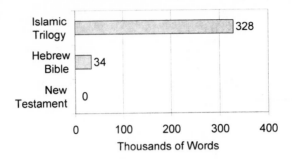

Words Devoted to Political Violence

Then there is the qualitative measurement. The political violence of the Koran is eternal and universal. The political violence of the Bible is for that particular historical time and place.

Here is a measurement of the difference. Jihad has killed about 270 million non-Muslims over the last 1400 years. Jewish political violence killed 300,000 (an order of magnitude surmise) since the days of the first Israel. As a comparison, jihad has killed thousands times more people than Jewish political violence.

These figures are not about moderate Muslims or extremist Muslims. These figures are about the doctrine that Muslims say is perfect. All Muslims, without exception, believe in the perfect Koran and the perfect Sunna. Now, how much of it they are aware of is another question. But the doctrine is there for all of us to see and study.

The violence in the Trilogy is for all Muslims, in all places and for all time. Jihad is to stop only when every Kafir submits. Look at Mohammed, the perfect example. He was involved with violence until the day he died. And on his deathbed he directed violence against the Kafirs when he said in his last breath: "Let there be neither Christian or Jew left in Arabia."

IF ISLAM IS SO VIOLENT, HOW CAN IT BE SO SUCCESSFUL?

The Sira records that when Islam committed violence, it attracted new followers. As Osama bin Laden says: "People like a winning horse." After 9/11 in the US, new followers joined Islam. Communism was a political system that preached, promised and delivered violence and it attracted many people. Many people love violence. Have you never paid any attention to Hollywood? Violence is piled upon violence and people line up to pay money to see it.

The success of most of Islam's growth can be attributed to high birth rates and immigration, not conversion.

THERE ARE DIFFERENT KINDS OF ISLAM

The differences in the various sects of Islam are due to religion, not politics. Take the Sunni/Shia split, its largest division. Both Sunnis and Shias completely agree on how to treat Kafirs and jihad. All Muslims subscribe to one of five schools of the Sharia and the Sharia's position regarding Kafirs and jihad is similar for all the sects.

The only big difference is when to use violent jihad or peaceful jihad against the Kafirs.

HADITH—SOME OF THOSE AREN'T REAL

If you quote a hadith to a Muslim and they don't like it, they will say, "Well, some of those hadiths are not acceptable (or not true or some other disclaimer)." Actually, when Muslims say this, they are practicing taqiyya, sacred deception and duality. If it is a hadith, then a Muslim cannot be denied the right to follow it. It is Sunna.

The hadiths cited in this book come from the very best collections—Al-Bukhari and Abu Muslim. These hadiths are the *creme de la creme* of hadiths and are called *sahih* (genuine) by top Islamic scholars. When Bukhari made his collection, he threw out 99% of those he found. Those 99% are the unsure ones, the other 1% that are used here are authoritative.

So the hadiths quoted here are genuine and real.

THE STORY OF THE ARABS, ABRAHAM AND ISHMAEL

The story of Abraham and Ishmael is told by Christians and Jews to authenticate Arabic culture and give it a tie-in to Kafir culture. It is usually a weak form of dhimmitude akin to the Abrahamic religions myth.

The core of the myth is told in the Koran about how Adam built the Kabah at Mecca. It was the first house of worship. Then Abraham brought Ishmael to Mecca, prepared to perform the sacrifice demanded by God. Ishmael was left in Mecca with his mother, Hagar.

Mohammed uses this myth to tie in the Arabs to the Jews. It was part of his early attempt to prove his prophet-hood by his being an inheritor of the Jewish tradition.

But the story of Arabs being the children of Ishmael and Abraham does not match with actual history. We find in the Sira a very detailed history of

Mecca at the time of Mohammed right down to the names of individuals, their children and wives. Arabs were very keen on family relationships. A person's very name gave you his father's or son's name and a chain of relationships. One of the things that infuriated the Meccans about Mohammed was that he said their ancestors were in Hell because they were not Muslims.

There must be a thousand names in the Sira and not a single person in Mohammed's Arabia is named Abraham, Ishmael, or Hagar. Not one. Why? They had no knowledge about any relationship between the Arabs and Abraham. The Arabs were deeply into genealogy and they knew of the Jews and Abraham, but they made no claim of kinship with their names. It was Mohammed who created the myth that all Arabs had blood ties to the Jews through Ishmael. Only after Mohammed did Jewish names become common amongst Arabs.

COULD I BE WRONG?

Once you know something about the doctrine of Islam, you can wonder if you really know that much when you hear some Muslim (or apologist professor) say that the Koran teaches:

- The Koran forbids compulsion in religion [2:256]
- The Koran teaches the oneness of god and acceptance of all the prophets [2:285]
- Brotherhood [49:13]
- Acceptance of diversity [5:48]
- Peaceful relations with the Jews and Christians [3:64; 29:46; 5:5]
- Universal justice and fair dealings with all people [4:135; 5:8]

When you hear this good teaching from some Muslim or apologist you may doubt your knowledge. Maybe you have misjudged the doctrine and there is some way that Islam can be a force for the good of humanity.

Before we examine how good a force the Koran is, let us examine how Islam is designed to deceive.

[Bukhari 4,52,267] *Mohammed said: war is deceit.*

Koran 4:142 *The hypocrites wish to deceive Allah, but He will deceive them.*

Koran 8:30 *Remember the unbelievers who plotted against you and sought to have you taken prisoner or to have you killed or banished. They made plans, as did Allah, but Allah is the best plotter of all.*

When it comes to deception, Mohammed was a deceiver and advised Muslims to deceive Kafirs. Allah plots against Kafirs and deceives them. All Muslims who follow the doctrine are deceivers of Kafirs. That is their sacred task. So when you hear about all of those good verses in the Koran, know that you are being deceived. All of the "good" verses in the Koran are denied later in the Koran. This is an example of the Mecca/Medina duality.

If Islam is so tolerant, why was there no one left to disagree with Mohammed by the time he died? When he re-entered Mecca as its conqueror, he issued death warrants for all those who had disagreed with him. Is this tolerance?

A supreme example of deception, taqiyya, is Imam Feisal Rauf's book *What's Right with Islam* in which he claims that the Constitution is based on Sharia principles and that Islam is based on the Golden Rule.

WHAT IS YOUR BASIS?

Instead of arguing against a point, ask the question: "Why do you say that? Where did you learn that?" In dealing with Islam, this is especially important as most people who speak will about Islam with you get their information from a magazine, web or TV. Islam is a text based doctrine that is all about Mohammed. Tell them that you want to hear what he did and said.

FILL IN THE BLANKS

It is a very useful technique to not oppose what your opponent/student says. Instead, give them the rest of the information. Fill in the other side of the duality. The beauty of this approach is that the other person is not being attacked at all, so they don't tend to push back and argue.

Islamic doctrine has two faces. When someone brings in some part about Islam that seems good, just give them the other rest of the story. If they talk about Meccan Islam, give them the other half, the Medinan Islam.

TRANSITION

This is not scientific reasoning, but it is a debate strategy. When you are first beginning to debate in person, you may find yourself in unfamiliar areas and feel you lack knowledge about something. If you are debating online or writing a letter to the editor, then you can research the facts, but in person you may, for tactical purposes, decide to change the subject by making a transition. Muslims do this all the time by changing the subject with an accusation against the Crusades, Christians or colonialism.

You can win an argument by rhetorical tactics. This is not scientific reasoning, but emotional reasoning. It works so well that you should always be aware of when it is used by others.

The technique is very simple—transition to Mohammed. It is always possible to move the discussion to Mohammed. For instance, if there is some talk about what is in the Koran, point out that the Koran repeatedly says that all Muslims must follow the prefect example of Mohammed. Once you get to Mohammed, you can move to abuse of women, hatred of Jews, violence against intellectuals and artists, slavery...

INSULTS

Don't ever attack the other person in any way. Don't raise your voice or insult. It never persuades and only makes the other person more angry and stubborn. All debate should be done from the angle of teaching and insults don't create a teaching moment. More than that, it shows you to be out of control and unprofessional.

If you are insulted, your response depends upon whether an apologist or a Muslim insults you. If a Muslim insults, thank them for being such a good Muslim and following the Koran and the Sunna. The Koran uses many insults and curses against Kafirs. Mohammed frequently cursed and insulted Kafirs. Insults are part of authoritarian reasoning and Islam. Thank them for showing how Islamic logic and reasoning work. Their next Islamic move should be to use some form of threat. Ask them if they want to display their threat by revealing it.

If they are not a Muslim, stay with the authoritarian thinking theme. Bring out that insults, name-calling and put-downs are part of authoritarian thought. Attack the fact that authoritarian thought is part of Official Islam, the Big Lie.

SECULAR MUSLIMS DON'T BELIEVE THE RELIGIOUS "STUFF"

First, why talk about individual Muslims? What does any individual prove about any group? If you know of a Christian who cheats, does that prove anything about Christianity? No. Don't discuss Muslims, except to point out that they come in three flavors—Meccan, Medinan, and Golden Rule. A Golden Rule Muslim is actually a Kafir, since he follows Kafir ethics, not Islamic dualistic ethics.

If they are a secular Muslim, then what part of the Koran and the Sunna do they reject and why? Good luck on getting them to deny any part of it.

WHY SHOULDN'T MUSLIM WOMEN WEAR THE HIJAB?

The hijab is a symbol of Sharia compliance. The Sharia is based upon duality and submission. Hence, the hijab is a symbol of hatred. The hijab is to the Kafir what KKK robes are to a black man—a symbol of the violent suppression of human rights. The hijab is a sign of support of Sharia law which includes the hatred of the Kafir and violence against them.

WHY IS PRAYER AT WORK NOT FINE?

Why should Kafirs submit to any Islamic demands? Freedom of religion does not mean the right to dictate what others do. Demanding to have special time for prayer is a political demand. If the Kafir does not allow it, then the Muslim does not have to pray. That is Islamic Sharia law. While prayer is religious, the demand on the Kafir is a political demand.

ISLAMIC VIOLENCE IS CAUSED BY POVERTY AND OPPRESSION

This statement is the same as saying: "I do not have the slightest knowledge about the Sunna of Mohammed and am completely ignorant about the Koran of Medina."

During the last nine years of his life, Mohammed averaged a violent event every six weeks. He is the perfect Muslim who is the perfect model of behavior. Muslims are violent because Mohammed was violent. Violence is pure Sunna and does not need anything from the Kafirs.

MODERATES CAN REFORM ISLAM FROM THE INSIDE.

Islam is the religious, political and cultural doctrine found in the Koran, Sira and Hadith. How does anyone reform any of the doctrine? Islam cannot change or be reformed according to its own doctrine. A Muslim can be reformed, but not Islam.

The Sira is comprised of 67% violence[3]. Only 21% of the Hadith is about jihad. The Koran devotes 64% of its text to Kafirs[4] and every reference is

3   http://cspipublishing.com/statistical/TrilogyStats/Percentage_of_
Trilogy_Text_Devoted_to_Jihad.html

4   http://cspipublishing.com/statistical/TrilogyStats/AmtTxtDevoted-
Kafir.html

bigoted, hateful and evil. How do you take this and reform it? No one can reform Islam.

The only reform a Muslim can offer is to not choose what is on the menu. This is what the so-called moderate Muslims do. The violence and hatred are in the doctrine, but they do not choose to accept it. But, they still defend Islam and deceive Kafirs about the true nature of Islam that they are avoiding. In other words, "moderate" Muslims are deniers and deceivers.

All moderates must be asked if they believe in the Koran and the Sunna of Mohammed. If they do then all the arguments in this section apply.

SHARIA LAW IS JUST LIKE JEWISH LAW.

Sharia law is based upon duality and submission. Sharia law expresses hatred for the Kafir and subjugates all women. Sharia law is designed for world conquest, subjugation, oppression and annihilation of all Kafir culture. Jewish law is about how to be a Jew and has no designs on non-Jews. Indeed, Jewish law states that the law of the land trumps Jewish law. Jewish law is not like Sharia law.

YOU ARE NOT A KAFIR; YOU ARE A PERSON OF THE BOOK

Muslims like to say this to Christians and Jews if they show knowledge about Kafirs. Kafirs believe that Mohammed was not a prophet. A person of the Book has to believe that Mohammed was the last of the prophets. A Christian has to believe that Jesus was not the Son of God, there is no Holy Trinity, that the Gospels are in error, and that Jesus was not crucified. Only if you hold these beliefs, then you are a real Christian, in the view of Islam. Otherwise, the Christian is just another Kafir.

A Jew has to believe that the Torah is in error and that only the Koran has the only true stories about Moses, David, Abraham and the other Jewish patriarchs. If, additionally, the Jew accepts that Mohammed is the final prophet of the God of the Jews, then such a Jew is a person of the Book and a real Jew (according to Islam). Otherwise, the Jew is simply a Kafir.

TREAT THEM AS A FRIEND

The process of educating others about Political Islam can only start with someone who has agreed to discuss Islam. When we speak one-on-one, the only winning method is to talk as to a friend. Never adopt a combative mode. Do not oppose and become emotional. Be a teacher. The dhimmi is a good person who is trying to do the right thing. They do not want to be a bigot and are terrified of being called a racist. They are filled with the media version of Official Islam. They went to school, even college, and they were taught the Official Islam and so it must be right.

Do not oppose them. Give them the added facts about the doctrine and relate everything from the Kafir point of view. For instance, what does it mean to Kafirs when a Muslim woman wears a burka or hijab? Teach them from the Sunna (as was done above); always give the story of Mohammed.

BRIDGE BUILDING AND INTERFAITH DIALOG

One of the most painful things is to watch ministers and rabbis go to interfaith dialogues with Muslims. The dhimmi religious leaders want to build a "bridge", but don't know the first thing about how a bridge is built. In the real world, when you go to build a bridge, you do survey work and learn about what both ends of the bridge will be built on. But the dhimmi bridge builders pride themselves on not knowing the first thing about the Muslim end of the bridge—not the first thing.

The dhimmis build one end for the bridge on their theology and ethics and the other end of the bridge is "tolerance", another word for saying that they will believe anything they are told by a Muslim and will believe nothing said by a Kafir. The bridges these religious dhimmi leaders build are based on fantasy. They are not building bridges, but are building rainbows. See how beautiful the illusion is?

A general condemnation of Christians, Jews, Hindus and Buddhists is that all the Kafir religions have reduced their doctrine to compassion and tolerance. That emotional quality is necessary, but it is also necessary to have knowledge and truth to go with it. Otherwise you wind up with idiot compassion. And that is what Christians, Jews, Hindus and Buddhists offer at interfaith dialogues—idiot compassion. They become useful idiots for Islam.

They find two or three things that seem to align with their doctrine and hope this makes everything all right.

In debating with such dhimmis, praise their desire for peace, but point out their lack of knowledge. They are basically narcissists, who see the argument revolving around their own goodness, not truth. Point out how self-centered they are and how true compassion would include learning about Islam as well.

Show them how Islam has attempted to annihilate all Kafir religions for 1400 years. Show them that the peaceful periods of co-existence are merely temporary rests before annihilation. Make them dwell on suffering of Kafirs. Point how Muslims never accept any responsibility for this suffering and deny it.

I HAVE SEEN MODERATE ISLAMIC WEB SITES

Someone surfs the web and finds a version of a kinder and gentler Islam. Why isn't that true? Isn't that hope?

The web site promises a tolerant and loving Islam, not like that terrible extremist Islam. This is the ultimate dream of all Kafirs. The dream is that moderate Muslims will forge a reformation. This dream ignores the simple fact that both the Wahabbis and the Taliban are reform movements. They do not dilute the doctrine found in the Trilogy. They really walk Mohammed's talk.

So why is the Wahabbi the real Islam and the kinder/gentler Islam not possible? Islam means submission. Muslim means one who has submitted. Islam is the cause; Muslims are the effect. Islam makes Muslims; Muslims do not make Islam. What a Muslim says about Islam is immaterial. There is only one authority, Mohammed.

The kinder/gentler Islam is based upon the Islam preached in Mecca for 13 years. This Islam was followed by the violent jihad of Medina. Two different Mohammeds, two different Islams. So the answer to reform is to use the Meccan Koran and Meccan Islam.

There is a problem, however. Islam is a process; it is not static. Mecca is the beginning part of the process. You can't just throw it out. Then there is the matter of the Koran clearly stating that the later Islam of Medina is the stronger, better Islam. The Medinan Islam is the completion of Islam—you can't throw it out.

There is another dreadful problem. The Koran is perfect. The Sunna (Mohammed's sacred pattern of the perfect life) is sacred. How can you reject what is perfect? That would mean labeling Medina as bad and evil. Rejecting Medina would also mean rejecting the code that the Sharia is based upon.

We must end our ignorance and learn about the doctrine and history of Islam. It is no longer hard to do that. The entire corpus of Koran, Sira and Hadith can be held in one hand and has been made easy to read. It is immoral to be so ignorant. Turn to Mohammed, not some imam. Then you will get the whole truth and nothing but the truth.

RADICAL ISLAMIC GROUPS

What does "radical" mean? Killing, robbing, enslaving, assassination, torture, deceiving, jihad? As long as those behaviors occur with the Kafirs on the receiving end, they are all acts that were performed by Mohammed. If Mohammed performed these actions, then they are not radical. Mohammed defines normative behavior for all Muslims.

What happened in Mumbai, India, the World Trade Towers and Beslan, Russia was not radical. Each and every action at those sites was based upon the Sunna of Mohammed.

MODERATES ARE USING THE KORAN TO PROVE THE RADICALS TO BE WRONG

Anytime anyone references only the Koran when they are talking about Islam, you are dealing with a deceiver or an ignorant person. The Koran is only 16% of the Islamic canon. The Koran does not have enough in it to accomplish even one of Islam's vaunted Five Pillars. The Sira and the Hadith compromise the 84% of Islamic canon that shows a Muslim how to be a Muslim.

The Hadith devotes 21% of its text to jihad[5]. The Sira devotes 67% of its words to jihad. Which "moderate" can deny those facts?

The Koran devotes 64% of its words to Kafirs, not Muslims. Out of all this material in the Koran, some of it in Mecca seems to promise goodness to the Kafir, but the later Koran takes away this chance of goodness.

The "radicals," the Medinan Muslims, are right. The Meccan Muslims are deceivers, perhaps of themselves, but certainly deceivers without any doctrinal basis.

Disregard what anyone says, except Mohammed. Actually, there is one, and only one, Muslim who will give you the straight truth and that is an apostate, one who has left Islam. But apostates say that no one believes them.

DON'T MALIGN ISLAM'S HOLY PROPHET

Since when is quoting from the Sira and Hadith maligning? Mohammed gave out the rules for rape in jihad. He owned sex slaves, told Muslims it was good to beat their wives, laughed when his enemy's heads

---

5   http://cspipublishing.com/statistical/TrilogyStats/Percentage_of_
Trilogy_Text_Devoted_to_Jihad.html

were thrown at his feet. It's in the book. Such behavior goes on for page after page, year after year. Why is referring to facts maligning?

THERE ARE FUNDAMENTALISTS IN EVERY RELIGION

We must be clear. All that matters is politics. Religion is prayer and Paradise and Judgment Day. These things don't concern us.

This statement assumes that Islam is comparable to other political systems and religions. What is remarkable is that this statement is only made by those who know nothing about the doctrine of Political Islam. They don't know Sunna from tuna—Mohammed is perfect. Every Muslim, without exception, is supposed to imitate Mohammed down to the slightest action. Is that fundamentalism? If so, then every Muslim is supposed to be a fundamentalist. It is the Sunna.

INTERFAITH DIALOGUE WILL LET US MEET MUSLIMS AND CHANGE THEM

So you change some Muslims, so what? Are you going to change Islam? No. Is a Muslim going to change Islam? No. Islam is found in the Koran, Sira and Hadith. That is not going to change.

You can reform a Muslim and make them an apostate, but you cannot reform Islam.

THE KORAN HAS LOTS OF PEACEFUL VERSES

What does that prove? There have been men who killed a wife in jealousy. The fact that the great majority of his life was good does nothing about his being guilty of murder for only a second.

Mein Kampf is only 7% Jew-hatred. That means that it is 93% good. Therefore, *Mein Kampf* is a good book. Do we have your logic down pat here?

NOT ALL MUSLIMS WILL DECEIVE YOU

No, and for many different reasons. But deceiving the Kafir about Islam is ethical. So why do you want to do business with someone who has a sacred directive to lie when it helps Islam?

Every Muslim has three natures—Meccan Islam, Medinan Islam and Kafir. If he is manifesting his Kafir nature and the Golden Rule, then he is honest. So honesty is proof of his Kafir nature, not his Islamic nature.

IT ALL DEPENDS ON HOW YOU INTERPRET IT

There is truth to the fact that there are many things in the Koran that depend upon interpretation. As an example, Muslims are to command good and forbid wrong. This comes from a verse in the Koran. Interpretation goes into exactly who does this and how they are to do it. But this is a religious matter.

However, the way that Kafirs are to be treated is not in this category. It is true that the Koran says two different things about how to treat Kafirs, there is both tolerance and jihad. But this is not a matter of interpretation. The tolerance is advised when Islam is weak, jihad comes when it is strong.

The interpretation argument is an attempt to deal with duality in the Koran. Usually, the interpretation argument is tied into saying that there are good and bad verses in the Bible. Today Jews don't use those violent verses to blow people up; they don't interpret it that way. So, if Muslims would just interpret the Koran in the right way, we could all get along.

But Muslims do interpret the Koran the right way according to Mohammed. The Koran is a dualistic document and that is what Muslims do. Some of them are playing good cop and a few play bad cop. Dualism reigns and the dhimmis pretend that the good cops will interpret the Koran the right way and change the minds of the bad cops. Not! The proper interpretation of Islam is that the bad cops outrank the good cops.

Another approach to interpretation is the Sharia. Sharia is the classical interpretation of Koran and Sunna by the finest Islamic scholars. As an example the Sharia says that jihad is killing Kafirs, not internal struggle. That is the proper interpretation of the Koran.

HOW TO USE THIS MATERIAL

All of these arguments amount to the same thing—use the doctrine of Political Islam to provide a complete picture of Islam.

When you read a chapter like this you can get verbal overload, since there are so many points. If you are debating online, then this chapter can be a reference. If you are persuading in person, then when it is over, reread this chapter. You will probably see new approaches that you can use the next time. Practice makes perfect.

GLOSSARY

When you learn new words you can think new thoughts. Islam is based on concepts that are totally foreign to us and to understand Islam, you need new words.

ablution, a ritual washing to become clean for religious acts.

abrogation, the Koran is filled with verses that contradict each other. The doctrine of abrogation is that the verse that is written later is better that the earlier verse.

Abu Bakr, Mohammed's closet Companion and his father-in-law, the first caliph.

Abu Talib, Mohammed's uncle, who adopted him, taught him how to be a caravan trader, and protected him in his role as a tribal elder. He died a Kafir and was condemned to Hell by Mohammed.

ahadith, the Arabic plural of hadith; hadiths is used in English.

Aisha, Mohammed's favorite wife of the harem. He married her at six and consummated the marriage at age nine. She was eighteen when he died. Many of the hadiths are from her.

Ali, Mohammed's cousin and son-in-law. He is considered the head of the Shia sect and was the fourth caliph (the first caliph, according the Shias).

Ansars, the Helpers. The Ansars were the first converts in Medina and gave money and shelter to the Muslims who left Mecca to come with Mohammed.

apostate, one who has left a religion, in particular, Islam. The Koran says that apostasy is the worst sin possible. It is far worse than mass murder. Mohammed and Abu Bakr killed apostates.

Black Stone, a dark stone, roughly seven inches in diameter. It is set into the corner of the Kabah. It was there before Mohammed.

caliph, a political and religious leader of Islam, roughly a pope-king.

circumambulate, to move in a circle around the Kabah while praying.

companion, one who knew Mohammed. When spelled Companion it refers to most important companions: Abu Bakr, Umar, Uthman and Ali.

Copt, Copts were the original Egyptians, their ancestors included the pharaohs.

dhimmi, a Kafir who is "protected" by Islam. A dhimmi has no civil rights, for instance, cannot testify in courts against a Muslim. Today, a dhimmi is a Kafir who defers to Islam, an apologist for Islam.

Five Pillars of Islam, praying five times a day; paying the zakat, the Islamic tax; fasting during Ramadan, going on pilgrimage to Mecca; and declaring that there is no god, but Allah and Mohammed is his prophet.

Gabriel, an archangel of Allah, who relayed the Koran to Mohammed.

ghira, absolute control of a woman's sexuality in all of its forms is part of a man's ghira (pride, honor, self-respect and sacred jealousy).

hadith, a Tradition, or small story, about what Mohammed said and did.

Hadith, a collection of hadiths.

haj, (hajj), the pilgrimage to Mecca.

Helpers, the first Muslim converts of Medina who helped the Muslims who came from Mecca, known as the Ansar in Arabic.

Holy Spirit, the archangel, Gabriel, in Islam.

Hudaybiya, an area near Mecca. It is famous because Mohammed was recognized as a political leader when he signed a treaty. It is important to Kafirs because Mohammed showed that Islam only enters into treaties when weak and will break them when it becomes strong.

imam, an Islamic religious leader of the Sunni sect.

immigrants, those who left Mecca with Mohammed.

isnad, the chain of witnesses who relayed a hadith. The source person must have personally heard and saw what they reported. The hadith were recorded 200 years after Mohammed's death, so there is a long chain of who said what to whom.

jihad, struggle, also fighting in the path of Allah. It is much more than killing or war. All effort for the supremacy of Islam is included. Writing a letter to the editor about Islam, making demands on employers or voting for a Muslim candidate are all jihad.

jinn, a conscious being on earth, made of fire. They can work for good or bad. The Koran says that some of them are Muslims.

jizya, a special tax on Kafirs in Islamic countries. In history texts it is called a poll tax and can be as high as 50% of the income.

Kabah, a stone building, cubic in shape, measuring about 30 feet on edge. The Black Stone is mounted in a corner. There is no Islam without the Kabah.

Kafir, a nonbeliever, a non-Muslim. The lowest form of life, cursed by Allah

mullah, an Islamic religious leader of the Shia sect.

poll tax, a tax per person, also known as jizya, that is paid by dhimmis. It can be as high as 50% of income.

prostrations, lowering yourself to the ground while praying, part of Islamic prayer.

Quraysh, Mohammed's tribe.

rightly guided caliphs, the first four caliphs—Abu Bakr, Umar, Uthman and Ali. They were very close to Mohammed.

Saed, one of Mohammed's close Companions. He gave the judgment that lead to the beheading of 800 male Jews.

Safiya, a Jewess who married Mohammed after he killed her husband, cousin and tortured her father to death.

Sharia, Islamic law based upon the Koran, Sira and Hadith. In it all Kafirs are second class citizens, at best. Islam has the goal of replacing our Constitution with Sharia law.

Shia, those who follow Ali, about 10% of Muslims, strong in Iran and southern Iraq. The differences between the Shia and the Sunni are mainly political. They willing to kill each other, but are united against the Kafirs.

spirit, the archangel Gabriel.

Sunni, those who follow the Sunna. They are about 90% of Muslims. The difference between Sunni and Shia is mainly political and is over who can be caliph.

Sunna, what Mohammed did and said is called the Sunna. It is the ideal pattern of Islamic life.

sura, a chapter of the Koran.

Sira, the life of Mohammed by Ishaq, *Sirat Rasul Allah*. It is one of Islam's three sacred texts, the Trilogy.

Sufism, a mystical form of Islam. It was adopted from Hinduism and Buddhism by conquered Kafirs who converted to Islam.

Torah, the first five books of the Old Testament.

Trilogy, the three sacred texts of Islam—the Koran, the Sira (Mohammed's biography) and the Hadith (what Mohammed did and said).

Umar, the second caliph. He created the Islamic empire.

umma, the Muslim political, religious and cultural community. A Muslim is a member of the umma, before his is a citizen.

Uthman, the third caliph, a close Companion of Mohammed. He was assassinated by Muslims.

zakat, a tax on Muslims, one of the Five Pillars. It is usually 2.5% of wealth.